Generative AI For Executives

A Strategic Roadmap for Your Organization

Ahmed Bouzid
Paolo Narciso
Weiye Ma

Apress®

Generative AI For Executives: A Strategic Roadmap for Your Organization

Ahmed Bouzid
McLean, VA, USA

Paolo Narciso
Seabrook Island, SC, USA

Weiye Ma
McLean, VA, USA

ISBN-13 (pbk): 979-8-8688-0949-1
https://doi.org/10.1007/979-8-8688-0950-7

ISBN-13 (electronic): 979-8-8688-0950-7

Managing Director, Apress Media LLC: Welmoed Spahr
Acquisitions Editor: Shivangi Ramachandran
Development Editor: James Markham
Coordinating Editor: Jessica Vakili
Copy Editor: April Rondeau

Cover designed by eStudioCalamar

Distributed to the book trade worldwide by Apress Media, LLC, 1 New York Plaza, New York, NY 10004, U.S.A. Phone 1-800-SPRINGER, fax (201) 348-4505, email orders-ny@springer-sbm.com, or visit www.springeronline.com. Apress Media, LLC is a California LLC and the sole member (owner) is Springer Science + Business Media Finance Inc (SSBM Finance Inc). SSBM Finance Inc is a **Delaware** corporation.

For information on translations, please e-mail booktranslations@springernature.com; for reprint, paperback, or audio rights, please e-mail bookpermissions@springernature.com.

Apress titles may be purchased in bulk for academic, corporate, or promotional use. eBook versions and licenses are also available for most titles. For more information, reference our Print and eBook Bulk Sales web page at http://www.apress.com/bulk-sales.

Any source code or other supplementary material referenced by the author in this book is available to readers on GitHub (https://github.com/Apress). For more detailed information, please visit https://www.apress.com/gp/services/source-code.

If disposing of this product, please recycle the paper

To our loved ones, everywhere.

Table of Contents

About the Authors...**xv**

Chapter 1: Unraveling the Basics of Generative AI..............................**1**

A Closer Look at Artificial Intelligence 2

    Traditional AI...3

    Generative AI 3

    Core Differences Between Traditional and Generative AI 4

    Traditional AI Pluses 5

    Generative AI Pluses 6

What Makes Generative AI So Compelling? 7

    Synthetic Data for Medical Imaging 7

    Predictive Analytics for Patient Monitoring 7

    Drug Discovery Acceleration 8

Core Concepts of Generative AI..8

    Generative Adversarial Networks (GANs).......................................8

    Transfer Learning 9

    Natural Language Processing (NLP) 9

    Conditional Generation 9

    Supervised Learning...10

    Unsupervised Learning...10

    Data Augmentation 10

    Hyperparameter Tuning 11

Business Solutions..11

    Sales and Sales Management 11

    Recruitment...13

    Talent Retention...13

    Corporate Finance 15

    Pricing 16

    Competitive Analysis 17

    Marketing Communications...17

    Customer Care and Support 18

    Customer Retention and Account Management 19

Conclusion 20

Chapter 2: Exploring the Transformative Potential of Generative AI 23

Data Analysis and Decision-Making...24

Examples..26

    Customer Sentiment Analysis for Product Improvement.............26

    Supply Chain Optimization for Cost Efficiency............................26

Operational Efficiency 27

    Examples 28

Strategic Planning and Risk Management..29

    Examples 30

Collaborative Work Environments 31

    Examples 32

Cost Reduction and Resource Optimization.......................................33

    Examples 34

Product and Process Innovation 35

    Examples 36

Conclusion 37

Chapter 3: Revolutionizing Content: Generative AI in Marketing and Advertising **39**

The Impact of Generative AI on Content Creation 40

Efficiency and Cost-Effectiveness 40

Improved Personalization & Targeting 40

Enhanced Creativity 41

Examples Where Generative AI Is at Work Now 41

Maintaining the Company's Voice with Generative AI 42

Importance of Brand Voice and Identity in Marketing 42

Strategies for Ensuring AI-Generated Content Aligns with Brand Values 43

Lean into Clarity with Generation Rulesets 43

Continuous Monitoring and Quality Control 43

Human Review Input Is Necessary 44

Examples of Companies Keeping Their Voice with AI 44

Putting the Marketing Team in the Driver's Seat 45

Addressing AI Concerns 45

Strategies for Empowering Marketing Teams 46

Integrating Generative AI into Marketing Workflows 48

Step-by-Step Guide for Integrating AI into Existing Marketing Processes 48

Best Practices for a Seamless Transition 49

Getting Started 51

Ethical Considerations and Challenges in AI Marketing 51

Addressing Ethical Concerns Related to AI in Marketing 51

Ensuring Transparency and Accountability 52

Strategies for Responsible AI Usage 52

Future Trends and Opportunities in AI-Driven Marketing 53

  Emerging Trends in AI-Driven Marketing and Advertising 54

Conclusion 57

Chapter 4: Elevating Customer Interactions with Generative AI 59

The Significance of Personalized Experiences 61

  Generative AI in Action: A Retail Example 62

  The Impact of Personalization 62

  Enhanced Customer Service 63

  Personalized Engagement...64

  Examples 65

The Impact 67

  Step 1: Identifying Opportunities for AI Integration 67

  Step 2: Selecting the Right AI Tools and Partners..68

  Step 3: Implementing with a Customer-Centric Approach............................68

  Step 4: Continuous Learning and Improvement 69

Use of Customer Data 70

Overcoming Technical Integration Challenges with Existing Systems 70

Preparing for Organizational Changes, Including Staff Training
and Shifts in Job Roles 71

  A Call to Action 72

Conclusion 73

Chapter 5: Streamlining Operations with Generative AI 75

Identifying Opportunities for AI in Operations 76

  Process-Mapping and AI-Readiness Assessment 76

  Priority Areas for AI Integration 77

  Generative AI Applications in Operations..77

Implementing Generative AI Solutions 78

Technology Stack and Integration 79

Vendor Selection and Collaboration... 79

Pilot Projects and Scaling... 79

Training and Change Management 80

Upskilling Staff 80

Change Leadership... 81

Optimizing and Iterating AI Use 81

Case Studies and Best Practices 82

Success Stories.. 82

Lessons Learned and Pitfalls to Avoid... 83

Evaluating AI Impact on Operations 83

Performance Metrics and ROI Analysis 84

Sustainability and Long-Term Benefits.. 84

Conclusion 84

Chapter 6: Harnessing Generative AI for Product Innovation 87

Generative AI in the Product Development Lifecycle 88

Ideation and Market Research... 88

User Research and Persona Development 89

Product Design and Prototyping... 91

Product Development and Testing... 92

Marketing and Launch... 94

Framework: The AI-Augmented Innovation Cycle..................................... 96

Overcoming Challenges and Ethical Considerations 98

Getting Started: Practical Next Steps 100

Conclusion 102

Chapter 7: Strategies for Successful Generative AI Implementation.....105

Assessing Organizational Readiness 106

Current Technology Landscape: Evaluating Existing Infrastructure.............. 106

AI Maturity Assessment: Determining the Organization's
Readiness for AI Integration 107

Gap Analysis: Identifying Gaps in Technology, Skills, and Processes........... 108

Developing a Clear AI Strategy.. 109

Vision and Goals: Defining the Vision for AI within your Organization 109

Use Case Identification: Selecting High-Impact, Feasible Use
Cases for Generative AI 110

Roadmap Creation: Establishing a Phased Implementation Plan 110

Investing in Technology Infrastructure 113

Data Management: Ensuring Robust Data Collection,
Storage, and Processing Capabilities 114

AI Tools and Platforms: Selecting Appropriate AI Platforms and Tools 115

Integration with Existing Systems: Strategies for Smooth
Integration with Your Current IT.. 115

Building a Skilled Workforce 116

Talent Acquisition: Hiring AI Experts and Data Scientists 117

Training and Development: Upskilling Existing Employees on
AI Technologies and Practices 118

Cross-Functional Teams: Creating Teams with a Mix of Technical and
Business Expertise 119

Fostering a Culture of Innovation 120

Leadership Commitment 120

Change Management: Managing the Organizational Change
Process Effectively 120

Encouraging Experimentation: Promoting a Culture That Embraces
Experimentation and Learning from Failures 121

Ensuring Ethical and Responsible AI Use 122

    Ethical Guidelines: Establishing Policies for Responsible AI Use................122

    Bias and Fairness: Implementing Strategies to Minimize Bias in
    AI Models..123

    Regulatory Compliance: Ensuring Compliance with Relevant Laws and
    Regulations...123

    Conclusion 124

Chapter 8: Navigating Risks and Legalities of Generative AI...........125

    Identifying Risks in Generative AI..126

        Data Privacy and Security..127

        Intellectual Property (IP) Issues...129

        Ethical Concerns...130

        Operational Risks 132

    Legal Frameworks and Regulations...133

        Current Legal Landscape..133

        Key International Regulations and Standards 134

        Future Legal Developments..134

    Mitigating Risks 136

        Implementing Robust Data Governance 136

        Ensuring Compliance...137

        Addressing Ethical Concerns...138

        Enhancing Operational Resilience 140

    Best Practices for Business Executives 141

        Risk Assessment and Management 141

        Legal and Ethical Considerations 142

        Continuous Monitoring and Improvement 143

    Conclusion 145

Chapter 9: Evaluating the Success of Generative AI Initiatives........147

The Challenge of Evaluating Generative AI...147

    Frameworks for Evaluating Generative AI 148

    Key Metrics for Evaluating Generative AI...150

Implementing an Evaluation Framework 152

    Case Study: Evaluating a Generative AI Content Creation Tool 153

Challenges and Considerations...155

Future Directions in Generative AI Evaluation 155

Conclusion 156

Chapter 10: Looking Ahead: Preparing for the Future of Generative AI 159

Capitalizing on Emerging AI Trends..160

    Strategic Technology Investment...160

    Quantum Computing: Opportunities for Competitive Advantage 160

    Neuromorphic Computing: Enhancing AI Capabilities 161

    Innovative AI Paradigms 162

Future-Proofing the Workforce...163

    Evolving Talent Management..164

    Redefining Roles with AI Integration 164

    Creating New AI-Centric Job Opportunities 164

    Continuous Learning and Development..165

    Implementing AI-Driven Learning Programs 165

    Incorporating AI Skills into Training Curricula...165

Building a Scalable AI Infrastructure..166

    Investing in AI-Ready Environments..167

    Strengthening Industry Collaborations 168

    Public–Private Partnerships for AI Advancements......................................168

    Collaborating with Global AI Research Entities..169

Unlocking New Business Opportunities 169

    AI in Emerging Markets 169

    Breakthrough Applications 170

Preparing for Market Disruptions.. 171

    Risk Management and Mitigation.. 171

    Agile and Adaptive Strategies.. 172

Sustainable AI Practices 173

    Ensuring Long-Term AI Sustainability....................................... 174

    Collaborative Innovation 174

Conclusion 175

Index..**177**

About the Authors

Ahmed Bouzid is founder and CEO of Witlingo, a McLean, Virginia–based startup that builds products and solutions to help brands establish and grow their voice and social audio presence. Prior to Witlingo, Dr. Bouzid was head of Alexa's Smart Home product at Amazon and VP of product and innovation at Genesys. Dr. Bouzid is an ambassador at the Open Voice Network and heads their Social Audio community. Dr. Bouzid holds 12 patents in the speech recognition and natural language processing field, and was recognized as a "Speech Luminary" by *Speech Technology* magazine.

Paolo Narciso is head of product and program development at the AARP Foundation, a Washington, DC–based national nonprofit. In his role, he develops and deploys solutions that build financial stability and social connections. He holds a doctorate in education from Creighton University and sits on multiple technology boards, advising on the use of blockchain in healthcare and to secure property rights for marginalized populations.

Dr. Wei Ma obtained her PhD in speech processing and recognition from Katholieke Universiteit Leuven (Belgium) in 1999 and has been practicing professionally in the speech recognition field since 1994. She has held several technical leadership roles in Unisys, Schneider Electric, and Convergys, and is now lead speech scientist at the MITRE Corporation, in charge of building speech systems for the Federal Aviation Agency.

CHAPTER 1

Unraveling the Basics of Generative AI

The term "artificial intelligence" (AI) represents a category of software systems that emulate tasks requiring human intelligence and cognition, from playing chess to diagnosing diseases and engaging in spoken-language conversations. This chapter explores the dynamic landscape of AI, dissecting the realms of Traditional AI and Generative AI.

Traditional AI, characterized by the explicit, rule-based algorithms implemented in traditional programming languages, is juxtaposed against Generative AI, which thrives on large datasets, likening data to rules. Delving into the core distinctions, the chapter contrasts Traditional AI with the creative, pattern-centric learning capabilities of the newly emerging Generative AI.

While Traditional AI is often seen as rigid and constrained, Generative AI excels in tasks requiring creativity and pattern recognition. In this chapter, our goal is to highlight, but without lapsing into hype, the revolutionary potential of Generative AI through real-life examples, such as synthetic data creation for medical imaging, predictive analytics in patient monitoring, and accelerating drug discovery.

After identifying and explaining the core Generative AI concepts that a business executive needs to be familiar with and understand, we provide concrete applications of using Generative AI to assist in business-critical tasks, including sales optimization, recruitment assistance,

© Ahmed Bouzid, Paolo Narciso, Weiye Ma 2024
A. Bouzid et al., *Generative AI For Executives*,
https://doi.org/10.1007/979-8-8688-0950-7_1

talent retention, and impacts on corporate finance, pricing, competitive analysis, marketing communications, customer care, and customer retention. The examples are meant not only to spark the imagination of the business executive on how to use Generative AI to solve specific problems they are facing, but also to help combat the prevailing false perception that Generative AI is nothing more than a mere "souped-up chatbot." Generative AI is a business-transformative technology that needs to be taken seriously by the business executive not only because it opens a whole world of efficiency and productivity, but also because anyone who elects to dismiss it as a fad is risking falling behind their competition, and doing so quickly and probably with little chance to recover, given the rapid speed of adoption by those who are natural early adopters of new technology.

A Closer Look at Artificial Intelligence

"Artificial intelligence," or "AI," is a term used to broadly refer to a class of software systems that execute tasks that are considered to require a nontrivial level of human intelligence and cognition. For instance, playing chess, we grew up thinking, requires uniquely human thought—and thought of the intelligent sort, no less. Diagnosing a disease is another example: Only a highly trained doctor can diagnose disease. Holding a spoken conversation using human language certainly would be categorized as an instance of artificial intelligence.

But one may ask: Well, what's the difference between software such as a spell checker or browser or a calculator and the software that powers an AI system?

Actually, the question is a very good one because it highlights the fuzzy meaning of "AI." The vast majority of software out there—even software that delivers high productivity or saves lives—today would not be considered AI for two reasons: First, the problems have been solved, once and for all, using fully deterministic rules (calculator) or data lookup (spell checker). Anything that is purely rule driven and will always give you the same answer given the same input is generally not considered AI. And second, the problems to solve are the type of problems that we thought only human beings could solve, either naturally (recognizing faces, understanding speech, creating music) or after extensive training and in collaboration with a highly educated or highly trained community and often by using specialized tools (for instance, disease diagnosis, project plan creation, text summarization, translation, and transcription of audio) .

For the purposes of this book, we will differentiate between two types of AI: Traditional AI and Generative AI.

Traditional AI

In a nutshell, Traditional AI is a methodology for building a software system by explicitly designing rule-based algorithms and then implementing those algorithms using a traditional programming language, such as Java, Perl, Python, and C, or languages built to implement AI, such as Lisp and Prolog.

So, for instance, a piece of software that converts temperature from Celsius to Fahrenheit, and vice versa, would be written using Traditional AI methods. We know the exact equation to use to convert from one scale to the next, so that, to get our answer, all we have to do is to provide a number as input and then get a number as output. And if we wanted, we could even verify manually to make sure that the software gave us the right answer.

Generative AI

In contrast, Generative AI is a methodology for building a software system by training it on a large amount of data that pertains to a domain within which we are seeking a solution. In a sense, data is to Generative AI what rules are to Traditional AI.

So, for example, a piece of software that has been trained on one million images of real MRIs of ailing kidneys and one million images of real MRIs of healthy kidneys would most probably be able to correctly— or at least to a very high degree of certainty—classify a brand-new MRI image of a kidney as either ailing or healthy. Another example would be training a system on tens of thousands of job descriptions and then asking the system to write a job description for a specific role described in one sentence. Music is another example: The system is fed with, say, thousands of hours of classical jazz music, and then, when asked, it can create a brand-new piece of classical jazz music that one would be hard pressed to distinguish from a piece that was generated by a human being.

Core Differences Between Traditional and Generative AI

To understand the core differences between Traditional AI and Generative AI, first note this: If one were to ask those who built a Traditional AI system to walk you through exactly the steps that were taken by the AI to deliver an output given an input, they would be able to walk you through (in fact, in software development the term is "step through") the steps, line by line, instruction by instruction, rule by rule, from beginning to end.

In sharp contrast, if one were to ask those who built a Generative AI system to walk you through exactly the steps that were taken by the Generative AI to deliver its output, the answer they would give you is, "I can't." They may describe the architecture and the strategy that the AI used, they may give you details about the data and the attributes that were used, may even explain how the data is labeled, and so forth, but for any given input, they would not be able to tell you exactly what the AI did to deliver the result. In other words, and in a real sense, the AI system is at least partially, if not completely, a black box not only to its users, but also to its very creators—the architects, the data scientists, and the developers.

Traditional AI Pluses

Traditional AI is often presented in contrast to Generative AI as dumb, constrained, and unexciting. In part, this is true: Traditional AI does rely on explicit rules coded up by human beings that, when executed, deliver nothing new, but exactly what the system was told to deliver. But it would be false and foolish, and even dangerous, to think that Generative AI systems are always superior to Traditional systems.

For one thing, Traditional AI is preferred in any setting where you want the system to be absolutely predictable and to adhere exactly to well-defined, enumerated, unchanging steps. For instance, if you need a system that ensures compliance with complex financial regulations and policies, Traditional AI is preferred. Such an AI can implement and enforce explicit rules to verify compliance, reducing the risk of regulatory breaches.

Another example would be making real-time decisions in manufacturing processes based on predefined rules. Here, Traditional AI is employed in manufacturing environments to make rapid decisions on the production line. For instance, systems can use predetermined rules to identify and address issues, such as adjusting machinery settings or flagging defective products.

A third example would be medical diagnostics expert systems. In certain diagnostic applications, especially those where well-established rules and heuristics exist, rule-based expert systems can outperform generative models. They can incorporate explicit medical rules and diagnostic criteria to assist healthcare professionals in decision-making.

But beyond the imperative of ensuring that the AI is predictable (and its output explainable and verifiable), in those instances where the rules are well known and, crucially, are stable and do not need to be adjusted frequently, building a Traditional AI system is often far cheaper than building a Generative AI one for two main reasons: (1) Programmers of such AI systems are readily available and affordable, while those who can build a Generative AI system are scarce and expensive; and (2) Large amounts of data would need to be gathered to deliver a Generative AI system, whereas such data would not be needed to build a Traditional AI system.

Generative AI Pluses

Generative AI offers several advantages over Traditional AI, especially in tasks that involve creativity and complex pattern recognition.

For instance, Generative AI systems are able to learn in ways that don't require humans to explicitly dictate what needs to be learned. Instead, the system is given a large number of examples of what to learn, and the system, using various techniques, is able to detect patterns, structures, and relationships between objects and attributes that will enable it to produce output—e.g., the answer to a question—that is based on what was learned but does not replicate in any guided way something that was programmed by a human. Such systems are especially useful when confronting phenomena that cannot be explained or described in any detailed way.

For instance, what rules does a musician, or a poet, or a painter follow in coming up with something new? To be sure, they follow the rules of their craft, and may adopt a style and set of techniques, as they are creating, but by and large, the creative output is as unexplainable to the artist as it is to anyone who beholds the piece of art. The output is the child of a whole world of past experience and the pressures of the moment. No rule-based system can be built to do that.

Another strength of Generative AI is its capacity to manage dynamic and evolving environments. Generative AI is especially useful in cases where data patterns change over time or where new data continuously influences the system's performance. Building a system that is periodically updated by simply feeding it a new batch of data and letting it learn and adapt can be done far more cheaply and quickly than with a Traditional AI system, which would require expensive human beings (experts in the field) to manually adjust (and test the validity of) their rules and programs.

What Makes Generative AI So Compelling?

The best way to communicate just how compelling Generative AI is as a technology is to share examples of real-life, life-saving problems that this technology—and only this technology, at least at the moment—can solve.

Here are the three such examples that we give when someone tries to dismiss Generative AI as a fad—and a dangerous one at that, often reducing the whole technology to a ChatGPT that gives wrong answers. But when we explain that Generative AI is much, much more than a "souped-up chatbot," as a detractor once put it, people quickly begin to understand that we are in the middle of a radically revolutionary moment.

Synthetic Data for Medical Imaging

Generative AI is being used to create synthetic medical images that closely resemble real patient data. Why is this critical? Because such data can be used to train machine learning systems for medical image analysis and thereby enhance the accuracy of diagnostic tools. And by enabling more extensive training, Generative AI helps in the early detection of diseases, such as cancer, resulting in timely, life-saving intervention.

Predictive Analytics for Patient Monitoring

Generative AI models can analyze very large datasets from patient records to identify patterns that help predict potential health issues, enabling healthcare professionals to intervene early and work with their patients to take measures to prevent the development of potential disease, or to intervene if the disease is in its early phases.

Drug Discovery Acceleration

Generative AI is revolutionizing drug research and discovery by enabling scientists to generate novel molecular structures for potential drug candidates. By analyzing vast datasets related to molecular interactions and properties, Generative AI can not only help expedite the identification of promising compounds, accelerating the development of new medications, but can also, by eliminating candidates that can potentially cause known adverse effects, minimize the potential of releasing into the market drugs that can have such effects on segments of the target population.

Core Concepts of Generative AI

Generative Adversarial Networks (GANs)

GANs are an architecture in Generative AI that consists of two subsystems—a **generator** and a **discriminator**—engaged in a competitive learning process. In a real sense, such a system is like a creative duo, where one member (the creator) generates content, while the other critiques it (the critic). The creator starts with basic creations and improves by learning from the critic's feedback. Simultaneously, the critic becomes adept at distinguishing real from fake. This dynamic competition elevates the skills of both the creator and the critic, with the creator constantly refining their creations to fool the discerning critic. Over time, this collaborative process produces astonishingly realistic and high-quality creations, making a GAN-based system a powerful tool for generating lifelike text, music, images, or even art.

Transfer Learning

Transfer learning is a technique used to speed up the development of a Generative AI system by leveraging the data and the models used to build a related AI system. We humans do this all the time. If, say, I knew how to fix motorcycles and wanted to learn how to fix cars, I would not throw away all of my knowledge about fixing motorcycles while learning how to fix cars; I would instead use it to help me learn faster. Similarly, with Generative AI, instead of starting from scratch for every domain and speciality, transfer learning lets the AI borrow useful information gained when developing for one domain to build a new one.

Natural Language Processing (NLP)

NLP in generative AI enables the creation of interfaces between humans and computer systems that respond to language in a way that makes communication between humans and computers more natural. Such systems help with tasks such as voice commands, language translation, summarization, text creation, and chatbots.

Conditional Generation

Conditional generation is the process of generating something that the AI was asked to generate through step-by-step instructions. An example would be telling the AI to generate an image of a large open field, and after it does so, asking it to put three trees on it, all equidistant one from the other, which it does, and then to place a large boulder in the center, with that boulder also equidistant from the three trees, and so on.

Supervised Learning

Supervised learning in Generative AI is akin to training an apprentice by providing it with examples of the object and the concepts you want it to learn. In the case of a virtual apprentice—in our case the AI system—it is providing it with labeled data, such as pictures of zebras and lemurs, and saying, "This is a zebra, and this is a lemur." The system then learns from these examples, allowing it to generate new images and other content following the patterns it detected and abstracted.

Unsupervised Learning

In contrast, unsupervised learning is more akin to giving, say, a child the freedom to explore and discover patterns and attributes on their own and without explicit direction and instruction. In the case of building an AI system, the AI would sift through unlabeled data and would identify hidden connections and structures without explicit predefined guidance.

Data Augmentation

It should be clear by now that the name of the game with Generative AI is data. The more data, the better. But collecting raw data is expensive, and at times the data collected may not have the variation of attributes that we need, such as variations in color, perspective, size, and so forth. By manipulating the images that we have, to create a subset of them by altering the color to include an underrepresented color, we can make the AI much more robust to real-life variation.

Hyperparameter Tuning

In machine learning, hyperparameter tuning is akin to optimizing a car's performance by adjusting external factors like tire pressure, fuel mixture, and suspension settings. Just as these tweaks impact a car's speed, fuel efficiency, and handling, hyperparameter tuning involves fine-tuning a model's external settings to achieve optimal results.

Business Solutions

So why should you, the business executive, care about Generative AI? Aside from using technologies such as ChatGPT in your own personal life, how can the use of this technology help either the bottom line or the top line of your business—or both?

Sales and Sales Management

Let's start with the most important function, as far as business owners, investors, shareholders, presidents, and CEOs of companies are concerned: Sales. How can Generative AI be used to help deliver better sales outcomes.

The secret to sales success is knocking on as many doors as possible. Period. In our current digital world, it means engaging as many potential buyers as possible. Key to delivering on that goal is minimizing the time that a sales person spends on engaging with a prospect. Such tasks include lead scoring, email outreach, generating responses to commonly asked prospect queries, writing notes after calls, scheduling follow-ups, and determining which opportunities to focus on and which to abandon. Generative AI can help with, or even outright do, many of these routine, mechanical tasks.

Imagine this: Every call your sales person makes is recorded, and after every call, the software transcribes the call, summarizes it, identifies the main takeaways and the next steps, proposes the exact next steps, logs this information in the CRM system that the sales rep is using (e.g., Salesforce. com), and even schedules in that CRM the follow-up task.

But beyond streamlining routine tasks, the AI can also help the sales representative and their manager ensure not only that they are focusing on the right opportunities, but also that they are not wasting time on opportunities that are unlikely to lead to success—whether through a close or beyond-the-close customer revenue growth (referred to as Lifetime Customer Value—or LTCV for short). The AI, for instance, can score an opportunity, wherever it may be in the sales cycle, by analyzing not only the deals that the sales representative was able to successfully close and those that they lost, but also the deals other members of the sales team won or lost. Further, the AI can also analyze those deals that were successfully closed with similar clients and score them for growth beyond close, deprioritizing them relative to prospects with a potentially higher LTCV.

For sales managers and executives, the core of their job is building and growing their sales team, and the twin banes of their existence are (1) Hiring the wrong people, and (2) Retaining the good ones. Generative AI can help on both scores. By analyzing the past performance of team members—which members succeeded and failed at what type of deals— the AI can not only score a given candidate's resume for likelihood of success but also provide questions to ask during an interview, the answer to which the AI can use to provide an even more reliable score. As for retention of those on the team who are performing, the mere fact that they are spending less time on tasks that keep them from engaging, speaking, and building relationships with prospects can help keep the sales rep happy because they are doing what they like to do naturally. But beyond that, one of the laws of sales physics is this: The more time you spend engaging prospects, the more deals you will close, and therefore the more money goes into the pocket of the sales rep. And as any sales manager and executive knows, what guarantees the happiness of a sales the horizon.

Recruitment

We touched on how Generative AI can help the sales manager and executive hire good sales people. But Generative AI can also help with recruitment for other business units.

First, the AI can help the recruiter put together an effective job description that will attract the right candidates to submit their resumes. We have all seen them, those boring, boilerplate job descriptions that no one really reads beyond a couple of bullets here and there. Imagine an AI that works collaboratively with the recruiter to craft a concise and readable job description that stands out as an interesting and even exciting invitation to join the team when compared to other job descriptions.

Beyond crafting compelling job descriptions, the AI can analyze historical hiring data—who was hired for what task, and who succeeded and who failed—to automatically score resumes and shortlist candidates whose qualifications align not only with the job specifications but also with past performance of previously hired employees. The AI may detect that, all else being more or less equal, those who have experience with customer care for a technology company are more likely to succeed as a sales representative. This type of correlation is precisely the kind of data point that is very hard for a human being to detect but is very easy for an AI to identify.

Talent Retention

We mentioned earlier how Generative AI can help with sales talent retention by enabling the sales representative to deliver results (i.e., close more deals and make more money for the company and for themselves) while doing more of what they love doing the most (interacting and speaking with prospects and building relationships) and less of those tasks that they find unpleasant and tedious and are not good at, but that are critical (taking notes, following up in a timely fashion, focusing on the right conversations, etc.) to ensure sustainable success. In other words: Help them be successful and happy at their job.

The same holds for all of the other business functions. You will retain your talent if your talent is not only successful at what they do, but also actually looks forward to working because it enables them to do the things that they love doing, day in and day out.

Key to the first—being successful at what you do—are knowledge and skill. If you know what you are doing, you will do it well. And the key to acquiring knowledge and skills is training.

The most effective type of training, as any teacher will tell you, is personalized training: Known to us as tutoring, where the teacher gets to know the student and fashions a strategy of teaching that takes into account the strengths and weaknesses of the student.

In a company with limited resources (and all companies have resources that are limited), personalizing the training for each team member is cost prohibitive. The training staff would not only need to spend time getting to know each person they train, but they would also need to build training paths that are tailored to the team member. This is assuming that the trainer knows how to tailor a training program to a team member's personal and professional attributes.

With Generative AI, given an assessment of the team member's knowledge about the company's mission, products and services, processes, and tenets (the AI can create a questionnaire of key questions based on the training material); previous job assessments from their managers, their peers, and those who report to them; and artifacts they may have created (copy they wrote, PowerPoint presentations that gave, emails they sent, transcripts of phone calls they made with clients or partners), the AI can come back with explicit recommendations on how to help the team member improve in their job. And a team member who is continually gaining knowledge, improving their skills, and gaining new skills is a much happier one than one who feels like they are not growing, not only as a professional but even as a human being.

Generative AI can also help detect instances of employee disengagement: Perhaps they are sending fewer emails, or the tone of their emails is much more subdued or more negative than usual, or they are taking more sick or personal days off than usual. Managers (because they are human) are notorious for being blind to, or in denial about, such patterns, or they may detect them when it's far too late and the employee has started looking for other opportunities elsewhere. Generative AI can be a partner in not only quickly detecting such patterns, but also forcing the manager to do something about it, since the warning would be issued to the manager and be on the record, so that inaction by the manager—if the employee does end up leaving—would need to be explained to the manager's boss.

Corporate Finance

A CFO, or chief financial officer, is the executive in the company who is tasked with managing the company's money, finding ways to save costs, maintaining accurate financial records, overseeing budgets, managing cash flow, and ensuring financial stability. The CFO also plays a key role in helping develop strategies to generate more revenue, ensuring the company's financial health and growth.

For instance, Generative AI can streamline routine financial chores, such as data entry, data reconciliation, and report generation. By automating such processes, the CFO and their team can focus their energies on more strategic and analytical activities..

Generative AI can also analyze large amounts of historical financial data, conduct scenario analyses, and generate forecasts, empowering the finance team to make more informed and accurate decisions than otherwise.

A third area in which Generative AI can help is developing and optimizing risk management strategies. By analyzing historical data about the company's performance and the performance of the competition, and by taking into account general market conditions and industry trends, the AI can identify potential upcoming risks and recommend mitigation strategies. This proactive approach could help the finance team anticipate and manage potential financial risks more systematically, enabling them to deliver a resilient and secure financial position for the organization.

Pricing

One of the basic tenets of life that a performing sales executive lives by is this: One should never lose a deal because of pricing. When you are engaged in negotiations with someone who is genuinely interested in your offering, the least intelligent thing you could do is to lose them because you could not get to a price that you are both comfortable with. A similar tenet should apply to marketing: You should not let pricing get in the way of someone who may be interested in your offering but doesn't want to start a conversation because they think you are too expensive for them.

Generative AI can help in many ways. First is dynamic pricing that helps you adapt the way you price your offer in real-time based on market conditions. Perhaps potential segments of your target market are doing well and have the budget to afford your offer and then some. Others may be going through a rough time, and even though they do want to buy, they can't afford your pricing. With dynamic pricing, you can adjust the price depending on the buyer, and do it in such a way that the offer itself varies, depending on the price point, to ensure that your offers remain profitable. If your offers are such that you can easily increase the list of features or capabilities or items on the offer list, or decrease it, at will, then you are more likely to trigger sales cycles.

Competitor pricing analysis is another area where Generative AI can be helpful. The AI could regularly monitor competitors' pricing strategies, enabling you to detect shifts and changes that your own analysis may have missed. In a sense, by having the AI keep an eye on the pricing of all your competitors, you are leveraging their analyses to inform your own actions and how to position yourself.

Competitive Analysis

Beyond keeping track of how your competition is pricing its offers, Generative AI can also enable you and your team to systematically and with minimal effort keep an eye on other aspects of your competitors: What new offers are they introducing, and what offers are they phasing out? What clients have they won lately, and what is being written about them in the press? Is their executive team changing, and if so, is this a signal that they are changing strategy and how they position themselves in the market?

Generative AI can easily do all of this today by monitoring information sources, such as your competitors' blog, their website, the press releases they published, or the podcast appearances of members of the executive team. Imagine receiving in your email, written in easy-to-digest language, a monthly report that not only provides notable information about the state of your competition, but also suggests actions and next steps to leverage the information gathered.

Marketing Communications

Of all the functions in any given business, marketing communications has been one of the earliest adopters of Generative AI products and solutions. This is hardly surprising, since the first Generative AI product that was introduced to the market that was highly usable and required no prior technical training was ChatGPT, an AI that specializes in the creation of narrative text. This provided marketers with the ability to not only create new content with minimal effort, but also to personalize that content depending on the target audience. Blog posts could now be created with a couple of prompts to ChatGPT, with the content creator's role now being that of an editor of text. Emails could also be created with a simple instruction to ChatGPT, such as invitations to webinars and answers to frequently asked questions from prospects.

Generative AI can also help the marketing communication team analyze social media trends and keep track of feedback posted in their various feeds. What videos are generating engagement and why; what posts seem to have hit a nerve and what do such posts have in common with each other; who are the influencers—whether detractors or champions—and how can such influencers be leveraged to promote the product to the right target potential buyers? Generative AI can do all of this today, and can do it well.

Customer Care and Support

Very much along with marketing communications, customer care and support has been one of the earliest adopters of Generative AI. And again, the reason has to do with the easy and affordable accessibility of ChatGPT.

In customer care and support, Generative AI has been used to great success in the creation of chatbots trained to answer not only the most frequently asked questions, but also any questions that are answerable given the content that was used to train the chatbot, such as FAQ pages, detailed support pages, training guides and manuals, webinars, podcast episodes, press releases, and blog posts.

Such bots, if they are built to the point where they are truly performing, can become partners with humans both for training purposes (the bot can ask the customer care and support trainee questions and help them learn and train themselves) and for when engaged in real-time conversations with customers. In fact, Generative AI has gotten to a point today where a support agent is speaking on the phone with a customer, with a Generative AI system listening in and suggesting answers to the customer care and support agent to either read outright or incorporate into their answer (or altogether ignore if the human agent deems the answer not useful).

Customer Retention and Account Management

The most tragic thing that can happen to a business is losing a customer who could have been retained with just a bit of due diligence. Customers do not like to switch vendors or alter their way of doing business. If they use your product and have incorporated it in their workflow, chances are that they will not switch to another product unless the pain of keeping your product is higher than the pain of adopting a new product that replaces yours, or even the greater pain of doing without a product at all.

Generative AI can help you identify customer pain points early on, perhaps even before the customer begins to express them as such. For instance, if your product is an online SaaS offering and you have customers who are using your product less frequently than before, perhaps that reduction in usage could be an indication of something that may lead them to leave your product. Perhaps after the initial swell of excitement using your tool, the user of the tool is not going back to use it as often as they should. This is a problem for you since by the time of contract renewal the decision may have already been made to terminate the contract, making it very difficult for your team to save the customer. Much easier would have been to detect the drop in usage and engage the customer to identify the cause: Is its business slowing down? Is it frustration with the product's features or its usability? If it's the first, you may want to be prepared to provide them an offer that better fits their budget, given the decrease in revenue. If it's the second, you may have the product managers do a deep dive on the discovered pain point and work to minimize or even eliminate the friction between the product user and your product.

Beyond spotting problems ahead of time and acting on them before they escalate to the next level of urgency, Generative AI can help your account manager identify clients who can benefit from new product features and offerings, allowing the account manager to cross-sell or upsell the client. Imagine an account manager starting their work day with all the clients they need to reach out to that day and what to engage them on, and imagine that any emails and conversations are fed back to the AI for recommendations on immediate follow-ups and other future actions.

Conclusion

The landscape of AI is dynamic and multifaceted, encompassing both Traditional AI and the transformative Generative AI. The dichotomy between explicit rule-based algorithms in Traditional AI and the data-driven, pattern-recognition prowess of Generative AI underscores the evolution of intelligent systems. While Traditional AI is methodical and linear, Generative AI's ability to learn without explicit human programming brings creativity and adaptability to the forefront.

Generative AI's significance is illuminated through real-life examples, illustrating its potential in solving critical, life-saving problems in medical imaging, patient monitoring, and drug discovery. We dispel misconceptions by showcasing that Generative AI surpasses the notion of a mere "souped-up chatbot" and stands as a revolutionary force in the technological landscape.

The business applications of Generative AI are vast, influencing sales outcomes, recruitment strategies, talent retention, corporate finance, pricing decisions, competitive analysis, marketing communications, customer care, and customer retention. Its integration into diverse business functions underscores its capacity to drive innovation, efficiency, and strategic decision-making.

As we navigate this radically revolutionary moment, it becomes clear that Generative AI is not just a trend but rather is a pivotal technology reshaping industries and redefining the possibilities of human–machine collaboration. It is clear that we have done nothing more than barely scratch the surface of what can be done with this new technology. The future holds the promise of continued advancements and impactful transformations, making Generative AI an indispensable tool for the effective 21st-century executive.

CHAPTER 2

Exploring the Transformative Potential of Generative AI

In chapter 1, we introduced the reader to some core concepts of Generative AI and shared a few examples to illustrate the immense potential that Generative AI holds for the business executive. But as the reader may have already guessed, we are barely scratching the surface. Indeed, we are still in the very early stages in the emergence of this technology to be able to detect, let alone flesh out, the problems that this technology can help us solve and the opportunities that it opens for us.

The aim of this chapter is to equip the business executive with the conceptual framework that will help them navigate their daily problem landscape and identify, given the deep knowledge they possess about their space, the way their company works, and the constraints they have to work with, specific, highly impactful opportunities where Generative AI can help them and their staff reach solutions and form initiatives. Within each section we'll provide a series of example cases that will help illustrate key points.

© Ahmed Bouzid, Paolo Narciso, Weiye Ma 2024
A. Bouzid et al., *Generative AI For Executives*,
https://doi.org/10.1007/979-8-8688-0950-7_2

Data Analysis and Decision-Making

Generative AI can significantly enhance data analysis and decision-making processes for business executives by providing valuable insights and streamlining complex tasks.

Imagine having a highly skilled assistant who will not only readily process vast amounts of data around the clock, but also synthesize meaningful information for you to help guide your decision-making.

First, Generative AI can help with the automation of data analysis, saving you and your team valuable time, effort, and resources. It can rapidly sift through large swaths of datasets and identify patterns, trends, and outliers at a breadth and a depth that might be challenging—or practically impossible—for a human to do anywhere as quickly, if at all. This then empowers executives to attain a comprehensive overview of their business landscape without getting caught up in the nitty-gritty of analysis and reporting.

Second, Generative AI can assist in predictive analysis. By analyzing historical data, Generative AI can generate informed forecasts about potential future trends, market dynamics, and even customer behavior if enough data exists. This ability to engage in informed forward thinking is invaluable for executives making strategic decisions, allowing them to be one step ahead of market shifts so that they can proactively adapt their business strategies.

Third is the ability of Generative AI to generate insights in a human-readable format. Experts are notorious for being bad communicators (perhaps deliberately to a certain extent to maintain their mystique and elevated status as a guru who dabbles in matters where mere mortals can't?), and the more of an expert they are, it seems, the worse their communication skills. Instead of confusing executives with arcane and intimidating jargon, complex charts, and graphs, the AI can cut to the chase and provide plain-language summaries, making it easier for non-technical stakeholders to not only comprehend what they see but, more crucially, to offer their perspectives and even act upon the information.

Generative AI also contributes to the optimization of decision-making by offering to the executive alternative scenarios and their potential outcomes. Good executives are not interested in one "final" answer to a question but rather seek alternative perspectives that they can learn from so that they can synthesize for the best possible outcome under the constraints that they are facing. In other words: Executives want options. By simulating different business strategies, for instance, executives are able to evaluate the impact of various decisions before moving toward the implementation phase. This "what-if" analysis helps mitigate risks by enabling the executives to identify the pluses and the minuses of each option, avoiding the risk of being blindsided by an aspect that, in hindsight, would be deemed an obvious failure in imagination.

In the area of customer insights, Generative AI can enhance an executive's understanding of their customer by analyzing direct customer behavior, feedback, transcripts of support calls, social media, and other unstructured data sources. It can generate actionable insights about customer sentiments and emerging trends, enabling executives to attain a deeper understanding of their target audience and enabling them to tailor products and services accordingly.

When it comes to resource allocation, Generative AI can help with the optimization of decision-making by recommending the most efficient distribution of resources based on available historical data and current market conditions. This ensures that budgets are allocated where they can yield the maximum impact for the business function or the company as a whole.

Additionally, Generative AI can enhance collaboration within an organization by facilitating communication between different departments and organizational functions. By providing insights in an easily readable manner, Generative AI effectively bridges the gap between technical (e.g., engineering, IT infrastructure provisioning) and non-technical teams (e.g., legal, HR), enabling true in-time collaboration to take place. The alternative, which is one of the banes of operating a business, is dealing with an expensive-to-resolve crisis that could have been easily averted.

Examples

The following examples show how Generative AI enhances data analysis and decision-making by providing actionable insights, predicting trends, and offering scenario-based alternatives, empowering executives to make informed choices and drive strategic initiatives.

Customer Sentiment Analysis for Product Improvement

Imagine you're the chief product officer tasked with overseeing the product suite of a consumer goods company. Generative AI can help you analyze customer feedback from various sources, such as online reviews, social media, and chat interactions. Using natural language processing, the AI would identify recurring themes and sentiments expressed by customers and inflection points of delight or disappointment. Instead of presenting executives with the raw data that is collected, the AI would summarize insights, such as "Customers by a wide margin do not like the new packaging and prefer the old one." This easily digestible piece of information enables executives to pinpoint specific areas for investigation, and potentially improvement, guiding product development and marketing strategies that are more likely to deliver business impact (more satisfied customers) than otherwise. In other words, by staying attuned to customer sentiments, executives can take informed action to enhance product offerings and maintain a healthy brand image.

Supply Chain Optimization for Cost Efficiency

Imagine that you are an executive who manages a manufacturing company. Core to your job is systematically tackling the challenge of optimizing the supply chain for cost efficiency. Generative AI can help by analyzing historical data related to supplier performance, production schedules, and transportation logistics. The AI could generate scenarios that outline for you the potential impact of different supply chain strategies, considering factors such as lead times, production costs, and transportation expenses. The AI could then suggest alternatives, such as adjusting the size of orders or diversifying suppliers, with projections on cost savings and corresponding potential risks. This information enables executives to make decisions that streamline the supply chain, reduce operational costs, and enhance overall efficiency.

Operational Efficiency

Generative AI can be a game-changer for business executives seeking to boost operational efficiency, helping them streamline processes, optimize workflows, and make smarter decisions that contribute to overall effectiveness.

Think of Generative AI as a digital efficiency expert. It can analyze your company's day-to-day operations and identify redundancies, bottlenecks, and optimization opportunities. In a sense, the AI acts as a seasoned operations manager, pinpointing where resources can be better allocated and where processes can be fine-tuned.

When it comes to decision-making, executives often face tough choices on how to allocate resources, whether it's time, manpower, or budget. Generative AI has the potential to step in like a wise advisor, providing insights on the most effective resource distribution based on data analysis. It can help ensure that every investment yields the best possible return, contributing to the overall efficiency and productivity of the organization.

Consider the day-to-day coordination and communication within your teams. For instance, Generative AI can enhance collaboration by acting as a bridge between different departments. It translates complex data into straightforward insights that various teams can understand, fostering smoother communication based on a shared vocabulary and a conceptual framework that all participants can navigate together. It's akin to having a universal translator for your business data, making collaboration possible and reducing the chances of frustration and misunderstandings, or worse, exclusion.

Furthermore, imagine the AI as an insightful navigator for supply chain management. It can analyze historical data, supplier performance, and logistics, and offer suggestions to optimize the supply chain for cost efficiency and other parameters that are important to management. And this doesn't have to be only about saving money, but can also be about ensuring that your products reach customers faster and with fewer hiccups. Generative AI helps executives make decisions that lead to a more streamlined and cost-effective supply chain, ultimately enhancing the overall operational efficiency of the company.

Examples

The following examples illustrate how Generative AI enhances operational efficiency by streamlining workflows, improving decision-making, and optimizing resource allocation, enabling executives to achieve greater productivity and effectiveness across the organization.

Streamlining Employee Onboarding

Generative AI can analyze data related to the onboarding process, identifying steps that may cause delays or confusion for new employees. By providing insights into how to optimize the onboarding workflow, the AI helps executives ensure that new hires integrate smoothly into the company, reducing training time and enhancing overall productivity.

Inventory Management for Retail

In the retail sector, Generative AI can analyze sales data, customer demand patterns, and supplier performance to optimize inventory levels. By suggesting the right quantities to order and the most efficient timing for restocking, the AI assists executives in preventing stockouts and overstock situations. This ensures that products are available when customers need them, reducing costs associated with excess inventory and missed sales opportunities.

In essence, Generative AI acts as a catalyst for operational efficiency, providing executives with valuable insights, enhancing decision-making, and contributing to the overall effectiveness of business operations.

Strategic Planning and Risk Management

Generative AI plays a crucial role in supporting business executives with strategic planning and risk management, acting as a reliable partner to navigate uncertainties and make informed decisions that align with the long-term goals of the organization.

Generative AI can act as a strategic guide that helps executives chart a viable, sober course for the future. It excels in analyzing vast amounts of data, identifying trends, and providing insights that are instrumental for strategic planning. This isn't just about forecasting; it's about having something akin to a trusted advisor who helps executives envision where the business should be heading and how to get there, given the data available and the patterns detected.

As we mentioned, one of the key contributions of Generative AI is its ability to simulate different scenarios. It's like having a crystal ball that allows executives to explore various pathways and understand the potential outcomes of different strategic decisions. This helps anticipate not only challenges but also opportunities, enabling executives to proactively shape strategies that are robust, resilient, and adaptive to dynamically changing market conditions.

Generative AI also steps in as a risk management ally. In the always-evolving business landscape, executives often grapple with uncertainties and the possibility of being blindsided. The AI acts as a risk scout, constantly looking out for and identifying potential pitfalls by analyzing historical data and evolving market trends. It assists executives in understanding the implications of the different decisions they may make—some of which the executives may already have been considering, while others may not have even occurred to them—allowing them to make choices that mitigate risks and enhance the overall stability of the organization.

Consider the task of entering a new market. Generative AI can analyze data related to market trends, consumer behavior, and regulatory landscapes. It provides executives with insights on the potential challenges and opportunities in the new market, aiding in the development of a strategic entry plan that minimizes risks and maximizes chances of success.

Examples

The following examples illustrate how Generative AI supports business executives in strategic planning and risk management, from market expansion strategies to product innovation, by providing data-driven insights and scenario simulations.

Market Expansion Strategy

Suppose an executive is considering expanding the company's market reach. Generative AI can analyze data from similar expansions in the industry, evaluating the outcomes and identifying key success factors.

By simulating multiple scenarios, the AI can help executives understand the potential risks and possible rewards associated with different expansion strategies. This insight could be invaluable in developing a well-informed market expansion plan that aligns with the organization's strategic goals.

Product Innovation and Development

In the realm of product innovation, Generative AI can help executives better assess the market demand for new products. By analyzing customer preferences, competitor strategies, and historical data on product launches, the AI can provide insights into potential risks and future opportunities. This could help executives make better informed decisions about investing in innovative products that meet market demands while at the same time mitigate the risks associated with new product development.

Collaborative Work Environments

Generative AI serves as a catalyst for fostering collaborative work environments, helping business executives enhance communication, teamwork, and overall productivity among their teams. Think of it as a collaboration coach with deep and broad knowledge not only about the company's domain, but also about the company itself and the individuals who make it run. Such a collaboration coach has the potential to consistently make possible a level of efficiency and cohesion in the workplace that would eliminate miscommunication, conceptual blind spots, and false assumptions.

One significant way Generative AI could contribute to collaboration is through improved communication. AI could act as a facilitator, translating complex data and insights into understandable language for diverse teams. This ensures that everyone, regardless of their technical background, can grasp the key information. It's like having a universal translator that promotes a shared understanding, reducing misunderstandings and promoting more effective communication across different departments.

Generative AI also excels at streamlining collaborative processes. It can assist in project management by analyzing data related to timelines, resource allocation, and task dependencies. For instance, by providing insights into potential bottlenecks or areas for optimization, the AI can help executives ensure that projects progress smoothly. This is akin to having a project coordinator that helps teams stay on track, meet deadlines, and work together more seamlessly.

Consider the task of brainstorming and ideation sessions. Generative AI can assist executives by analyzing data on market trends, customer feedback, and industry innovations. By generating insights and potential ideas, it acts as a creative collaborator, sparking inspiration and providing valuable input during brainstorming sessions. And since the suggestions are coming from an AI, the fear of offending a human colleague by rejecting such ideas is no longer an obstacle. Such a combination of free flowing and uninhibited ideation has the potential to deepen and widen creativity, fostering a more collaborative and innovative work culture.

Examples

The following examples demonstrate how Generative AI enhances collaborative work environments by improving communication, streamlining processes, and fostering creativity, helping executives build more cohesive and productive teams.

Cross-Functional Collaboration

In a scenario where different departments need to collaborate on a project, Generative AI can help bridge the communication gap. By translating technical data into plain language, it can facilitate collaboration between teams with diverse expertise. For instance, in a product development project involving both engineering and marketing teams, the AI ensures that both sides understand each other's priorities and contributes to a more harmonious collaboration.

Virtual Team Collaboration

In the context of remote work and virtual teams, Generative AI can enhance collaboration by providing real-time insights and updates. It could act as a virtual meeting assistant, summarizing key points, action items, and decisions and plans proposed and made during virtual meetings. This ensures that team members who couldn't attend the meeting live or those in different time zones are able to stay informed. In this way, the AI promotes a more inclusive and collaborative virtual work environment by facilitating seamless communication and coordination.

In essence, Generative AI functions as a collaborative ally for business executives, promoting effective communication, streamlining processes, and contributing to a culture of innovation. By leveraging its capabilities, executives can cultivate a work environment where teams collaborate more efficiently, share insights seamlessly, and collectively contribute to the success of the organization.

Cost Reduction and Resource Optimization

Generative AI can play a pivotal role in assisting business executives with cost reduction and resource optimization, potentially acting as a savvy financial advisor to guide decisions that enhance both the top and the bottom lines as well as the overall efficiency of the organization.

Generative AI can act as a virtual cost-cutting partner by digging deep into your operational data. It can identify areas where resources, whether they be time, money, or manpower, could be used more efficiently. It's akin to having a keen-eyed financial analyst that spots opportunities to trim unnecessary expenses and ensure that every investment yields maximum potential value.

One of the key contributions of Generative AI is its ability to analyze historical data and provide insights for smarter decision-making. By examining past trends and performances, the AI assists executives in understanding where resources have been most effectively utilized and where there may be room for improvement and optimization. This is akin to learning from the financial history of the company to make more informed decisions about future resource allocation.

Consider the process of supply chain management. Generative AI can analyze data related to suppliers, production schedules, and transportation costs. By identifying areas for improvement and suggesting more cost-effective strategies, the AI acts as a supply chain optimization consultant. This ensures that resources are allocated in a way that not only minimizes costs but also maximizes the efficiency of the entire supply chain.

Examples

The following examples highlight how Generative AI supports cost reduction and resource optimization by identifying inefficiencies, streamlining operations, and enhancing productivity, helping executives make informed decisions that maximize organizational value.

Operational Streamlining for Cost Reduction

Imagine you're an executive looking to cut operational costs. Generative AI can analyze data on various operational processes, pinpointing areas where tasks can be streamlined or automated. By providing insights into how workflows can be made more efficient, the AI assists executives in reducing operational expenses while maintaining or potentially even improving productivity and increasing efficiency, and maybe even introducing a culture of frugality throughout the workflow chain. This could involve optimizing internal processes like order processing, inventory management, or customer service, resulting in significant cost savings and greater customer satisfaction.

Employee Productivity and Time Management

In a scenario where executives aim to optimize employee productivity, Generative AI can analyze data related to work hours, project timelines, and task completion rates. By providing insights into time management and identifying potential bottlenecks, the AI assists executives in optimizing work schedules and resource allocation. This ensures that employees are working on tasks that align with organizational priorities, improving overall productivity and contributing to cost reduction.

Product and Process Innovation

Generative AI can serve as a dynamic partner for business executives in driving product and process innovation, acting as a potential catalyst for creative thinking and efficient development. Imagine it as a collaborative innovator that contributes fresh ideas and streamlines the innovation journey.

One of the key ways Generative AI facilitates innovation is by analyzing vast amounts of data to uncover insights that spark creative ideas. It's like having an innovation scout that explores customer preferences, market trends, and industry innovations. By distilling this information, the AI provides executives with a foundation for ideation, ensuring that innovation efforts are always grounded in a deep understanding of market dynamics and customer needs.

Generative AI can have a material positive impact on the ideation phase of product and process innovation. It can simulate various scenarios and generate potential ideas for new products or improvements to existing processes. But this isn't just about brainstorming; it's about having a creative collaborator that contributes to the generation of practical, data-driven ideas. It helps executives engage in free-flowing exploration of different avenues and possibilities, fostering a culture of innovation within the organization.

Consider the task of developing a new product. Generative AI can assist executives by analyzing customer feedback, market trends, and competitive landscapes. By providing insights into what features or attributes customers are looking for, the AI acts as a product development guide. This ensures that the new product aligns with market demands, increasing the chances of success.

Examples

The following examples demonstrate how Generative AI drives product and process innovation by uncovering customer insights, generating creative ideas, and optimizing workflows, enabling executives to cultivate a culture of continuous improvement and market relevance.

New Product Features Based on Customer Insights

Suppose you're an executive aiming to enhance an existing product. Generative AI can analyze customer feedback, reviews, and market trends to identify areas for improvement. By generating insights into what customers appreciate the most and what they find frustrating, the AI can help decision-makers innovate product features and enhancements, and even anticipate future frustrations given past behavior and feedback from customers about similar products. This could involve adding functionalities, improving user experience, or addressing pain points highlighted by customers, ultimately contributing to a more competitive and innovative product.

Process Optimization for Efficiency

In the realm of process innovation, executives may seek ways to optimize internal workflows. Generative AI can analyze data related to operational processes, identifying bottlenecks and areas for improvement in the product ideation and development process. By generating insights into how product roadmapping can be streamlined or automated, the AI can help executives innovate in internal workflows. This could involve adopting new technologies, revising protocols, or implementing efficiency measures, leading to enhanced operational efficiency and overall process innovation.

In short, Generative AI serves as a guide for executives navigating the realms of product and process innovation. By providing insights, sparking creative ideas, and contributing to the ideation process, the AI can accelerate innovation efforts and ensure that such efforts are grounded in a robust understanding of market dynamics and customer needs. Executives leveraging Generative AI can thus foster a culture of free-flowing innovation, driving the development of products and processes that position the organization for sustained success, growth, and profitability.

Conclusion

Generative AI is rapidly emerging as a multifaceted, multilayered ally for business executives, offering transformative benefits across various dimensions of organizational management. Its effectiveness in data analysis and decision-making present executives with a distinct strategic advantage over those who are lagging in the adoption cycle of Generative AI, providing not only insights but also a streamlined approach to handling complex tasks that would be difficult, if not impossible, to deliver through human-only effort. In the realm of operational efficiency, Generative AI is proving to be a game-changer by optimizing workflows and contributing to overall effectiveness.

Moreover, Generative AI's role in strategic planning and risk management can be business critical, offering a reliable go-to partner in navigating uncertainties and aligning decisions with long-term organizational goals. As a catalyst for fostering collaborative work environments, Generative AI facilitates enhanced communication and productivity, transforming teamwork into a more cohesive and efficient process.

The financial acumen of Generative AI shines through in its contribution to cost reduction and resource optimization, acting as a shrewd financial advisor that can guide executives toward decisions that positively impact the bottom line.

Lastly, in the pursuit of innovation, Generative AI emerges as a dynamic collaborator, fueling creative thinking and contributing to the efficient development of both products and processes. In essence, Generative AI stands as a versatile toolset, empowering business executives to navigate complexities and drive success across diverse aspects of organizational management.

CHAPTER 3

Revolutionizing Content: Generative AI in Marketing and Advertising

While the mainstream work world has become quite familiar with generic artificial intelligence (AI) platforms, such as ChatGPT, for example, there is far more that is worth serious consideration by companies and marketing programs than a simple responsive database system with text answers. Indeed, Generative AI provides a robust portfolio of material that can be used for video, music, art, and photography, expanding the fast and powerful reach of AI well into the visual and audio side of interactive communication.

Generative AI works on the same principles as generic AI: A user inputs variables and descriptive criteria, and the system scans its data repositories for the best fit, returning a response. However, unlike a text approach, Generative AI can produce compelling content that appeals to the non-literary audience, which has proven repeatedly to have a far greater marketing reach, decade after decade. It's the reason magazines, and then television, and in the 21st century internet streaming have taken center stage in marketing efforts.

© Ahmed Bouzid, Paolo Narciso, Weiye Ma 2024
A. Bouzid et al., *Generative AI For Executives*,
https://doi.org/10.1007/979-8-8688-0950-7_3

The Impact of Generative AI on Content Creation

Generative AI is already being worked on by *six out of ten marketing teams*, especially those on the cutting edge. However, unlike super IBM computer technology, Generative AI is accessible and affordable. More important, it has exponential reach for the investment put into it. It's beyond time to get started and access what that potential is for your company. The following sections explore some of its advantages.

Efficiency and Cost-Effectiveness

The Generative AI option delivers a gateway into impactful multimedia content *without the prohibitive cost* of actual production through traditional experts.

Whether hiring a professional photographer, artist, or video production team, the expenses involved can be in the hundreds of thousands of dollars for the end product, which may not be on target after all is said and done. The second problem with traditional marketing prior to AI was that it was extremely hard to quantify ROI metrics. The phrase, "We'll see when we get there," was a common, scary response.

Now, with Generative AI, a company can try out and test different marketing approaches without the pain of lost spending, focusing instead on desired demographics and producing far more accurate results with marketing campaigns.

Improved Personalization & Targeting

Many companies have had to settle for choosing one target market over the other due to the preceding issues. Instead, Generative AI easily allows a marketing campaign to hit multiple targets with different triggers and

40

attributes without driving up production expense significantly. That *flexibility produces a broader reach*, and it is also increases the number of niche-market penetrations that can be done simultaneously. Coordinated together, the same business could easily penetrate multiple markets with the same campaign and different visual elements via Generative AI. Additionally, the easy tailoring of the system allows for quick and effective response to feedback loops, improving ongoing market retention efforts.

Enhanced Creativity

Utilizing Generative AI, a company can quickly and efficiently produce marketing content with a variety of options, themes, and strategies for a fraction of the production expense, allowing a management team to see a far greater portfolio of options to consider. Even then, the company could still ultimately use professional production in the end, but with a clearer concept versus guessing and facing a costly disappointment.

Examples Where Generative AI Is at Work Now

Heinz Ketchup played on the idea that the initial forays into the business use of AI wasn't quite accurate. Working up a YouTube video on the premise of "asking AI" what it thought ketchup was with text prompts, the Generative AI example exhibits a simple but effective marketing position for Heinz Ketchup by "reinforcing" the idea that even AI doesn't hallucinate on quality ketchup. AI accurately produces images of Heinz.

Remember the kids' toy store, Toys"R"Us? While the physical stores disappeared, the company still exists online. The same venture engaged with Generative AI with a *marketing storytelling approach*, regenerating interest in the store as well as its lore. Reaction has been notable, especially on the aspects of what is real versus generated.

Dove's marketing team flipped the tables on arguments that AI might be biased due to its underlying dataset. Instead, the company *leaned into the idea* and generated a moving commercial video using Generative AI to show beauty is far more expansive and varied, just like the real human race.

Notably, all three of these projects started with creative human teams augmented by the power of Generative AI, not replaced by it.

Maintaining the Company's Voice with Generative AI

Generic AI tends to be the "voice" of the tool. In comparison, current iterations of Generative AI have improved tremendously, and personalized, accurate performances appear with increasing frequency in today's digital landscape with very unique brand associations. Effective communication pieces, eyebrow-raising video, and music media have become very hard to discern as artificial. Further, companies that have embraced the tool are pushing the envelope of what can be done with Generative AI and marketing the same with their brand at the forefront, particularly in the areas of idea visualization and prototyping of new technology. *Robotics continue to be the most recent example* that immediately comes to mind. In short, brand retention with AI is easy; it's only limited by the creator's imagination in application.

Importance of Brand Voice and Identity in Marketing

Why does brand association matter? Good ideas and trends go viral very quickly, especially online. However, if the brand association is not clear and present up front, that viral audience attention takes off without knowing clearly who has provided the benefit, and they go seeking it elsewhere. That leaves a wide-open channel for competitors and substitutes to run right in and take over a new market.

Strategies for Ensuring AI-Generated Content Aligns with Brand Values

Lean into Clarity with Generation Rulesets

Right from the start, content creation teams and marketing support should be working from an unambiguous ruleset promoting the company's brand. Templates that provide text, logos, music, images, and similar should all be set in stone so there's no confusion on application. Instead, all creative work focuses on how to add, expand, and enhance the brand identity with new product development. The rulesets can also take care of style choices, tone, and scenario applications, again ensuring consistent voice and presence every time the AI tools generate a new content option. Doing so limits "left-field" content from sneaking in, and it creates a minimum benchmark for all content that may be reviewed for release to the public.

Continuous Monitoring and Quality Control

That said, turning everything over to automation and rulesets alone would be a mistake. Content generation should continue to be monitored for aberrations and one-offs. Even the latest Generative AI is not perfect and will occasionally produce a hallucination in output. Regular checking, testing, and monitoring proactively catches issues before they become digital embarrassments. Remember, mistakes go viral just as fast as intended content that works great. However, prevention is cheaper than market-loss damage control after the fact.

Human Review Input Is Necessary

Technology can do a lot today, but it's nowhere ready to think like a human with experience in a company, product line, and, ultimately, a viable, moving market. That comes *with skill, time, and human thinking* in the moment for decision-making. Many of those aspects can be built in as parameters for conditions, but they still come from a human being with time under their belt doing the job. *Human review* should always be applied in content creation before going live, even when developed by Generative AI. It provides the best of both worlds—experience and the exponential speed of AI response.

Examples of Companies Keeping Their Voice with AI

Among companies that have leaned into branded AI, *Viator has been one of the notables* leading the charge. The company works regularly under the wing of TripAdvisor in the development of digital ads. Partnering with Greatrix, Viator established its brand with a solid, quantified reaction in record time.

The *Washington Post* has been utilizing Heliograf for years, but starting in 2020 it switched to story-telling with the tool, opening up new audience markets interested in audio news versus just reading and visual. The project successfully established AI-written stories for spoken word, realigning the paradigm of spoken news and podcasts.

ASOS provides an example of how rulesets can be applied effectively, maintaining its youthful voice and perception of its brand consistently across various projects.

Putting the Marketing Team in the Driver's Seat

Talk about AI in the office, and some listeners might have a visceral reaction similar to that when robots and computers were introduced on the factory floor: "Jobs are going to be replaced!" Not automatically true. While there is no question that Generative AI produces content that creates competition for work provided by professionals, it still takes company experts to know how to use that content effectively and build it into marketing campaigns. This is where placing the marketing team in charge is critical; it removes apprehension of job loss and instead refocuses energy on production.

Addressing AI Concerns

Addressing concerns around AI requires understanding its true impact on job displacement while recognizing the significant advancements in its capabilities.

Where Is the Job Displacement in Reality?

Companies that put their existing marketing teams in charge need their people to keep Generative AI momentum going at pace. Reliance on external contracts and procured resources become less necessary, and it's those suppliers finding themselves first displaced by the use of the tool. Additionally, freelancing and third-party support thrive on unaddressed gaps in organizational operations; where one need is no longer present, they shift to fill others. In the meantime, companies retain their own experience skillsets and *expand skillsets further with the addition of Generative AI*.

Skepticism: AI Is Not as Good as the Real Thing

The original output from the first versions of AI were absolutely lacking. These programs were essentially overhyped expansive databases basically designed to regurgitate the closest record resembling criteria from a user's criteria. That said, in only a few years, AI developments have leaped Grand Canyons in quality and capability, particularly in Generative AI. Now, content is being produced that is adequately able to challenge human-made product and, more important, it does it faster and in greater quantity than normally possible.

Strategies for Empowering Marketing Teams

To empower marketing teams in the adoption of Generative AI, companies can focus on strategies that alleviate anxiety through training, foster collaboration between tools and people, and encourage a culture of learning from mistakes.

Train Away Anxiety

The number one way that anxiety in a company adopting AI can be lessened considerably is through immediate training. Pushing marketing teams into upskilling programs with Generative AI immediately communicates two things. First, it tells people they are going to be using a new tool; second, it tells them they will have value being the ones expected to operate the tool. Otherwise, why would anyone be trained in the first place? Companies invest in resources and activities for growth and enhancement of output from existing commitments.

Collaboration of Tools & People

A well-proven approach with a new tool paradigm has been promoting synergy between people, skills, experience, and that new tool. By proactively pushing the use of Generative AI, i.e., moving people off the branch to fly immediately, the adoption rate increases dramatically out of necessity. There is no time for fear; people just start working with it immediately. That does come with some risks as well as delays due to adjustments, but overall positive adoption happens far faster than letting use of a new tool happen passively. Soon enough, resident experts begin to appear, and that allows a company to move into the next phase of Generative AI.

Encourage Mistakes Innovating versus Negative Adaption

People learn by doing, which means there are going to be moments of mistakes and goofs applying a new tool to existing expectations. That said, by learning in real-time what doesn't work well, people end up wasting less time and achieving better results faster. So, practice and exposure go hand-in-hand with advanced AI performance and output. Learning curves will always take some time to overcome, but the changes seen in companies taking on Generative AI definitely argue the mistakes are worth it.

Generative AI Is a People-Driven Tool, Not the Opposite

Again, people and Generative AI create a powerful synergy. Everyone involved simply needs to lean in hard and commit to making it work. Marketing teams that gyrate on anxieties of what-ifs lose time, productive energy, and eventually skill as people leave for perceived career protection. Companies can head off this panic by moving teams into training and upskilling right away, messaging investment and growth versus fear of replacement.

Integrating Generative AI into Marketing Workflows

The how-to part of bringing Generative AI into a marketing team and their processes comes into play with real-time application. Generative AI should never be an outside tool run by someone else; it should be a hands-on resource that the marketing team itself uses to produce content, revise it, tweak it, and refine it. Doing so not only produces home-grown content, but also helps teams speed up their learning of how to best use AI for their given company's needs.

Step-by-Step Guide for Integrating AI into Existing Marketing Processes

Integrating AI into existing marketing processes involves a step-by-step approach that starts with assessing current workflows, selecting the right tools, and using pilot testing to refine and enhance AI adoption effectively.

Assessing Current Workflows and Identifying Opportunities for AI

Borrow from project management and IT system development when it comes to integrating Generative AI with a marketing team. Assess one's current program and how it operates before implementing any kind of new change. Then, with the "as-is" status thoroughly documented, a "gap analysis" for where a company wants to be with AI integration can be applied. This two-step assessment and goal definition is critical. The gap analysis helps identify the practical ways Generative AI will actually be applied by the team.

Selecting the Right AI Tools and Platforms

There are already lots of tools associated with AI, many specific to certain types of technological response. That's where the project management step becomes so important. It immediately narrows the field to what should be most applicable for a marketing team versus generic AI. Tool alignment contributes significantly to adoption success, especially when a marketing team is already using technology extensively.

Pilot Testing and Iterative Improvement

Pilot testing new AI tools alongside existing practices provides a very vivid comparison a company can work with. Yes, there is a bit of redundancy involved, but the lessons learned on what Generative AI provides differently via a specific tool can make procurement decisions easy afterward.

Best Practices for a Seamless Transition

A seamless transition to using Generative AI in marketing requires best practices that ensure data privacy and security, establish measurable KPIs for success, and incorporate continuous feedback and improvement to stay ahead in a rapidly evolving landscape.

Ensuring Data Privacy and Security

A company implementing Generative AI with its own marketing needs to use a type of AI that can be kept private and secure from open-ended databases yet still enjoy the power of modern AI. This protects copyright assets and avoids premature leakage of content.

In addition to internal tool controls, marketing teams need to be trained on keeping their content development private. Communication should be through secure access systems, and AI systems should be reviewed for problems or privacy risks regularly (audits). Between best practices education and periodic audits, a good amount of content protection can be had with very low effort.

Establishing KPIs and Measuring Success

Metrics and key performance indicators also help ensure the efficiency of investments in Generative AI. By applying expected goal metrics to AI-driven campaigns, companies can keep their marketing teams and tools accountable. Instead of being adventures into the unknown, a common problem with traditional marketing, new campaigns created with Generative AI can have expectations clearly defined, such as impacts rates, population reaches, distribution rates, and web traffic, among other metrics. Marketing teams shouldn't be afraid of metrics with AI; instead, they should embrace them as targets to beat. Doing so helps push AI teams harder—with better results.

Gathering Feedback and Making Continuous Improvements

Once a system is in place, a company shouldn't just put the marketing team in neutral and forget about the implementation. Instead, there should be a regular review and feedback-loop process to see what can be refined and improved. Keep in mind, AI in general is still fairly new and going through significant design improvement. There is a strong likelihood that the Generative AI available five years from now will be significantly better than what is used today. Companies should welcome new applications within testing controls to safely integrate new ideas, tool versions, and application methods too. Being stuck on the same process simply ends up being a fast path to obsolescence.

Getting Started

Focus on defining how it will be used first, then apply it with a pilot approach, and finally refine regularly with feedback improvement loops. That combination will produce a viable marketing team supported by AI.

Ethical Considerations and Challenges in AI Marketing

Companies that are transparent about their use of Generative AI enjoy a couple of advantages right away. First, they avoid the accusation of trying to dupe their customers. Second, they don't seem to be coming across as trying to earn a "hard day's work" for nothing; people are sensitive to someone's cutting quality corners. Finally, concerns of marketing fraud are avoided, especially where it could otherwise be suggested, and then the company is in serious damage control mode trying to stave off a social media nightmare spurred on by an unfounded suggestion.

Addressing Ethical Concerns Related to AI in Marketing

All AI currently works off of pre-existing content. So, it is important to know what that content is versus blindly using AI tools and then expecting them to automatically be objective in output. Where a company is building Generative AI with its own data, steps should be taken to make sure that the dataset is as inclusive as possible. Otherwise, data biases can and do skew results.

Ensuring Transparency and Accountability

As noted earlier, being clear early on about the use of any AI in marketing is an advantage. The last thing a company wants is to be seen as being fraudulent in ads or awareness campaigns. So, it should be a *principled part of a marketing team's strategy* to always integrate AI awareness. Companies should wear their AI use as a badge, showing their markets how it gives them an advantage. Whether with data, imagery, content, or decision-making process, AI transparency strengthens public image.

Strategies for Responsible AI Usage

Responsible AI usage in marketing involves implementing ethical guidelines, conducting regular audits, and engaging with stakeholders and customers to ensure alignment with company values, compliance, and sensitivity to audience needs.

Implementing Ethical Guidelines and Frameworks

The usage of AI comes with incredible power to create, but it also includes the intensity of responsibility. A company's marketing team should already have its principles of use spelled out well before engagement occurs. These rulesets can easily provide predetermined guidelines for how to use AI with the company brand and messaging, and also to maintain privacy and be accountable in creativity. One of the best places to start involves the *IEEE's Ethics in AI Guidelines*. Another option is the *European Union's AI Ethics Guidelines*. Both provide a welcome framework that any company can build on.

Regular Audits and Assessments

Discussed in earlier segments, it's not enough to lay out principles; they need to be regularly monitored to ensure that the company's expectations with Generative AI are compliant. Creative sparks have a habit of spinning off when left to their own devices, so periodic audits help remind marketing teams that monitoring is active. This provides a company the benefits of prevention, ethical alignment, and staying within regulatory boundaries where they may apply.

Engaging with Stakeholders and Customers

Feedback loops with customers and stakeholders help tremendously, especially when refining the original work provided by a marketing team. Feedback helps narrow targets with accuracy, identifies sensitive areas to avoid, and shows the company has a concern about the interests of its customers and stakeholders. There are a variety of ways to pull in this valuable information: surveys, website forms, social media forums, focus groups, and more. Not only does feedback show genuine interest in connections with customers, it also provides a very low-cost form of marketing research teams can use repeatedly.

Future Trends and Opportunities in AI-Driven Marketing

AI continues to evolve, especially in the reach and power of Generative AI. As that evolution occurs, the capability of marketing will stretch further as well. The tool already finds itself at the edge of marketing innovation, promoting company growth and opening new markets. So, it makes sense for a company to also know what to expect with Generative AI going forward.

Emerging Trends in AI-Driven Marketing and Advertising

Emerging trends in AI-driven marketing and advertising include personalization at scale, advanced predictive analytics, voice and conversational AI, automated content creation, and advanced visual and video content generation, all of which are reshaping how businesses engage with their audiences and prepare for the future.

Personalization at Scale

Generative AI increases the scale of reach with effective cost control, two immediate benefits that make it immediately attractive. However, even more important, Generative AI allows instant flexibility for options and variations that otherwise take weeks to produce through other channels. That speed to market is powerful, and it only stands to increase with new technological breakthroughs in AI.

Advanced Predictive Analytics

The marketing field is far more than just ads and sales pitches. Marketing analysis and research matter just as much for successful campaigns, especially now when the digital world moves so much faster. AI has already been applied in *analytics tracking online behavior*, customer decision-making, likely successful promotion paths for traffic, and campaign success likelihood modeling. Additionally, Generative AI can easily combine with these in targeting what content will have the most resonance with target groups as well. Through probability and filtering, Generative AI becomes a very effective scalpel penetrating new markets otherwise untouched by general marketing.

Voice and Conversational AI

Generative AI positions well in customer web interface bots that provide user help and support, typically delivering after-sales assistance 24/7. Because the tools already have the ability to respond to variable input, they become a natural for after-hours customer support. However, simple text or robot responses turn people off. With Generative AI, there's much more of a human feel to the response, even if it is still AI providing the actual help. No surprise, successful integration of Generative AI in customer support has been growing fast.

Potential Future Applications of Generative AI

Development players heavily involved with the improvement of Generative AI are aggressively pushing the envelope closer to the truth and are very comparable to human-produced product. The music and audio industry is now feeling its presence the same way graphics production was impacted. Video improvements manifesting alternative options for content products are appearing as well. However, the more likely path for Generative AI involves *multi-media engagement with customers* based on their choices of contact via the internet (omnichannel marketing).

Automated Content Creation

The next step of Generative AI's producing content on its own without human prompts sits just around the corner, namely dubbed "agents." Companies may very well find in a few years that they can simply install tools that consistently produce content 24/7. This frees up marketing teams to focus heavily on strategy, identifying new markets and thinking about new ideas while the AI tool pushes out regular material already within channels defined. The automation approach reduces maintenance costs significantly and reroutes valuable resources to strategize for new opportunities.

Advanced Visual and Video Content Generation

Prompt-driven A/V content is already possible and improving. While early forays had many of the same glitches as basic AI did, rapid improvements are already visible, improving content development accuracy and reducing "oddball" material slipping in. The constant scale and speed of development works much faster, allowing the improvement cycle to operate faster than human experience–based improvement. It won't be much of a surprise to soon see movie-length content being developed that can compete with high-quality traditional production as well.

Preparing for the Future: Staying Ahead of the Curve

To stay ahead of the curve, companies should focus on several key areas.

Investing in AI Talent and Training

Marketing teams should take a close look at their current hiring expectations and revise them for AI. Generative AI expertise will be a necessity, especially with a solid understanding of programming and how to apply new iterations of tools as they come online. That also includes knowledge and fluent capability in all related digital skills, such as image editing, audio and video editing, web design, server management, and similar. Ignoring this aspect will create bottlenecks in team capabilities as AI becomes more and more a core process in marketing.

Fostering a Culture of Innovation

While companies with large structures tend to discourage thinking off the range, that's exactly where Generative AI marketing teams should be operating. Creativity is the bread and butter of pushing AI usage to higher levels of quality output. This is where soft-skill areas of psychology, sociology, anthropology, and similar come into play, honing content based on cultural norms and any new patterns emerging. People respond to what they recognize as familiar; content should be culture based to connect better as well.

Keeping Up with Regulatory Developments

External changes in how business uses Generative AI continue to be discussed and will likely show up as the tool enters industries more and more. The Hollywood-generated fear of computers taking over the world (i.e., the Matrix) continues to manifest any time that technology moves another step into daily life, and that fear can manifest in requests for laws to constrain it. Companies should seriously consider being active in such AI discussions, showing people and stakeholders how Generative AI is actually applied to help dispel misinformation. Simply waiting for government to find the right path on its own could very well be a mistake. Instead, by proactively showing people how AI benefits them and commerce, regulatory development can end up being far more positive in application.

Conclusion

Generative AI is revolutionizing marketing by offering a whole new world of possibilities beyond text-based interactions by tapping into music, video, and visual content to captivate the interest and imagination of broader audiences. Unlike traditional AI, which at best mimics human-like responses, Generative AI produces original, diverse, and impactful content tailored to specific demographics, resulting in cost-effective, personalized, and targeted campaigns with more precise bottom-line ROI. Indeed, Generative AI empowers marketing teams to experiment creatively while maintaining brand identity and control, ensuring authenticity and engagement.

Companies must of course balance automation with human oversight in order to navigate ethical concerns and considerations and to prevent unintended biases. By integrating AI into workflows with deliberation and care, and by training teams and embracing innovation, organizations can unlock new growth avenues and stay ahead of evolving trends. As Generative AI continues to advance, the potential for even more sophisticated content creation and engagement strategies will only grow, making this moment a uniquely opportune time for companies to harness Generative AI's capabilities, giving them a competitive edge in the dynamic marketing landscape.

CHAPTER 4

Elevating Customer Interactions with Generative AI

In today's rapidly evolving digital landscape, businesses are continually seeking innovative ways to enhance customer satisfaction and loyalty. The advent of artificial intelligence (AI), and more specifically Generative AI, has opened new avenues for transforming customer interactions into personalized and efficient experiences. This chapter aims to demystify how Generative AI can be a gamechanger in your customer engagement strategy, even if you're not deeply familiar with AI technologies.

Generative AI refers to a subset of AI technologies that can generate new content, responses, or data that were not explicitly programmed. Unlike traditional AI, which operates within the confines of predefined rules and datasets, Generative AI learns from vast amounts of data, identifying patterns, preferences, and behaviors. It then uses this understanding to create responses or content in real-time, tailored to the individual needs and contexts of each customer. This capability marks a significant departure from the one-size-fits-all approach, enabling a level of personalization and responsiveness that was previously unattainable.

© Ahmed Bouzid, Paolo Narciso, Weiye Ma 2024
A. Bouzid et al., *Generative AI For Executives*,
https://doi.org/10.1007/979-8-8688-0950-7_4

The goal of this chapter is twofold. First, we aim to illustrate the immediate benefits that Generative AI can bring to your customer service and engagement efforts. Through 24/7 availability, instant responses, and personalized interactions, businesses can significantly enhance the customer experience, leading to increased satisfaction and loyalty. Second, we provide a practical roadmap for integrating AI-driven customer interactions into your business. This includes identifying opportunities for AI integration, selecting the right tools, implementing these solutions with a customer-centric approach, and continuously improving based on feedback and AI's learning capabilities.

By the end of this chapter, you will have a clear understanding of how Generative AI can elevate your customer interactions through personalization and efficiency. You will be equipped with the knowledge to begin exploring and implementing Generative AI solutions in your customer engagement strategies, even if your current familiarity with AI is minimal. This is not just about keeping pace with technological advancements, but also about seizing opportunities to redefine customer engagement in ways that resonate with the modern consumer's expectations for personalized, efficient, and seamless experiences.

In essence, the transformative potential of Generative AI in customer interactions lies not only in its technological capabilities, but also in its ability to foster deeper, more meaningful connections with your customers. As we delve into the specifics of Generative AI applications and implementation strategies, remember that at the heart of these innovations is the opportunity to enhance the human experience, building stronger relationships between your business and your customers.

As we delve deeper into the realm of artificial intelligence, it's crucial to understand the distinction between Traditional AI and Generative AI, especially in the context of customer interactions. Traditional AI operates on a model where it's programmed to respond based on a finite set of rules and data. This means its responses are only as varied and insightful as the data and rules it was trained on. While effective for straightforward tasks and queries, this approach often falls short when nuanced or highly personalized responses are required.

Generative AI, meanwhile, represents a significant leap forward. It employs advanced machine learning models, such as generative adversarial networks (GANs) and transformers, which are capable of analyzing and learning from vast datasets. These models can understand patterns, preferences, and the nuances of human language, enabling them to generate responses or content that are contextually relevant and highly personalized. This ability to "create" rather than merely "retrieve" information allows Generative AI to provide solutions, suggestions, and interactions that feel remarkably human and tailored to the individual needs of each customer.

The Significance of Personalized Experiences

In today's digital age, customers expect more than just transactions from their interactions with businesses. They seek experiences that are relevant, convenient, and tailored to their individual preferences and needs. Personalization, therefore, has become not just a competitive advantage but also a necessity. Studies and surveys consistently show that personalized experiences lead to higher customer satisfaction, increased loyalty, and, ultimately, greater business success. Customers are more likely to return to platforms that remember their preferences and make relevant recommendations, creating a positive feedback loop that benefits both the customer and the business.

Generative AI in Action: A Retail Example

Consider the case of a retail company specializing in outdoor gear. Traditional AI might offer customers generic product recommendations based on popular items or broad categories like "hiking" or "camping." While useful, these recommendations may not resonate with every customer, leading to a missed opportunity for engagement.

Enter Generative AI. By analyzing a customer's previous purchases, search history, product reviews, and even social media activity, Generative AI can craft highly personalized recommendations. For instance, a customer who recently bought a tent and searched for winter camping tips might receive recommendations for a high-quality sleeping bag designed for cold weather, along with a personalized guide on how to choose winter camping gear. This recommendation is not just relevant; it's timely and shows an understanding of the customer's specific interests and needs.

Furthermore, Generative AI can generate engaging product descriptions, suggest complementary products, and even create personalized marketing messages that resonate with the individual's preferences. This level of personalization transforms the customer experience from a simple transaction to a curated journey, making the customer feel understood and valued.

The Impact of Personalization

The impact of such personalized experiences is profound. Customers are more likely to engage with recommendations that reflect their interests and needs, leading to higher conversion rates and increased sales. Moreover, the feeling of being understood and valued fosters customer loyalty and advocacy, which are invaluable in today's competitive market.

Generative AI's ability to understand and respond to customer needs in a nuanced and personalized manner marks a new era in customer engagement. By leveraging Generative AI, businesses can not only meet but exceed customer expectations, creating experiences that are not just transactions but meaningful interactions that build lasting relationships.

The distinction between Traditional AI and Generative AI lies in their approaches to dealing with customer data and queries. While Traditional AI can efficiently handle routine tasks, Generative AI excels in creating personalized, context-aware interactions that cater to the unique preferences of each customer. In a market where personalization is key to customer satisfaction and loyalty, the ability of Generative AI to deliver such experiences is a gamechanger for businesses aiming to thrive in the digital age.

The adoption of Generative AI within customer service and engagement channels heralds a new paradigm, offering immediate benefits that address both the operational challenges businesses face and the evolving expectations of modern consumers. Two primary areas where these advantages manifest most clearly are in enhancing customer service and personalizing customer engagement.

Enhanced Customer Service

One of the most significant benefits of integrating Generative AI into customer service operations is the ability to provide continuous, 24/7 support. Traditional customer service models, heavily reliant on human agents, face limitations in availability and scalability, often leading to increased wait times outside business hours. Generative AI, conversely, operates independent of time constraints, ensuring that customers receive assistance whenever they need it, regardless of time zones or holidays. This round-the-clock availability not only boosts customer satisfaction by meeting their expectations for instant support but also positions your business as reliable and responsive, a critical differentiator in today's competitive landscape.

In an era where time is a precious commodity, the expectation for instantaneity in customer service interactions has never been higher. Generative AI excels in providing immediate responses to customer inquiries, significantly reducing wait times that are often associated with human-operated service desks. By instantly processing and understanding the customer's request, Generative AI can generate accurate and relevant answers, addressing queries with efficiency that human agents might struggle to match. This capability not only enhances customer satisfaction through speed but also improves the overall efficiency of customer service operations, allowing human agents to focus on more complex, high-value interactions.

Personalized Engagement

The true power of Generative AI lies in its ability to understand and adapt to individual customer preferences, enabling a level of personalized engagement that goes beyond the capabilities of Traditional AI. By analyzing data from various touchpoints—past purchases, browsing history, customer service interactions, and even social media engagements—Generative AI can identify patterns and preferences unique to each customer. This deep understanding allows businesses to tailor their interactions, recommendations, and services in a way that resonates with the customer, fostering a sense of personal connection and understanding that is highly valued in today's market.

Beyond just recognizing customer preferences, Generative AI can dynamically adjust its communication style to match the customer's tone, mood, or previous interactions. This adaptability makes interactions with AI feel more natural and human-like, significantly enhancing the customer experience. For instance, if a customer expresses frustration, Generative AI can adopt a more empathetic tone, whereas for straightforward inquiries, it might maintain a concise, informative style. This dynamic interaction capability ensures that customers don't just receive personalized content but also experience a personalized communication style, further enriching the customer engagement process.

The immediate benefits of using Generative AI in customer service and engagement are clear. By providing 24/7 availability and instant responses, businesses can meet the modern consumer's expectations for immediate, accessible support. Simultaneously, by understanding customer preferences and dynamically adjusting interactions, companies can offer a level of personalized engagement that significantly enhances the customer experience. These advancements not only lead to increased customer satisfaction and loyalty but also position businesses to thrive in a highly competitive digital landscape. Through the strategic implementation of Generative AI, businesses can transform their customer service and engagement models, paving the way for a future where personalized, efficient customer interactions are the norm, not the exception.

The transformative impact of Generative AI on customer service and engagement is perhaps best illustrated through real-world applications across diverse industries. Two compelling case studies—a fashion retailer and a bank—highlight how Generative AI can be leveraged to offer unprecedented levels of personalization and efficiency, fundamentally changing the way businesses interact with their customers.

Examples

Retail Example: Fashion Retailer

Imagine a fashion retailer that has integrated Generative AI into its online platform. This technology sifts through vast amounts of data, including customer style preferences, past purchases, and current fashion trends, to offer personalized outfit recommendations. For instance, when a customer, who has a history of purchasing minimalist clothing, visits the retailer's website, the Generative AI system analyzes this data in real-time and curates a selection of outfits that align with minimalist aesthetics, considering factors like seasonality and the latest trends.

This level of personalization extends beyond mere product recommendations. The AI system crafts personalized emails and notifications that feel uniquely tailored to each customer, mentioning specific items they viewed but didn't purchase, suggesting complementary products, or offering styling advice based on recent purchases. This approach not only enhances the shopping experience by making it more relevant and engaging but also significantly increases the likelihood of purchases, as recommendations are highly aligned with individual preferences.

Banking Example: Personalized Financial Advice

Consider a bank that employs Generative AI to power its customer service app, providing personalized financial advice to its users. By analyzing a customer's financial history, spending habits, and long-term goals, the AI system can offer tailored advice that feels both personal and practical. For example, for a customer aiming to save for a home purchase, the AI could analyze their spending patterns and suggest a detailed savings plan, highlighting areas where they could cut expenses or recommending specific financial products offered by the bank that align with their saving goals.

This personalized financial advice extends to real-time interactions. When a customer contacts the bank with a query about investment options, the Generative AI system can instantly pull up their financial profile, consider their risk tolerance and investment goals, and provide recommendations that are tailored to their specific circumstances. This not only makes the customer feel understood and valued but also empowers them to make informed financial decisions based on personalized, data-driven advice.

The Impact

In both examples, the implementation of Generative AI has led to a significant enhancement in customer experience and engagement. The fashion retailer sees higher conversion rates and increased customer loyalty, as shoppers appreciate the personalized recommendations and feel that the brand truly understands their style. Similarly, the bank's customers benefit from customized financial advice that helps them achieve their financial goals, fostering trust and loyalty toward the bank.

These case studies underscore the potential of Generative AI to transform customer interactions across industries. By offering a level of personalization and efficiency previously unattainable, businesses can not only meet but exceed customer expectations, paving the way for deeper relationships and sustained business success. Through the strategic use of Generative AI, companies can redefine the customer experience, setting a new standard for engagement in the digital age.

Integrating AI-driven customer interactions into your organization requires a thoughtful, structured approach to ensure that the technology enhances rather than disrupts your customer experience. By following these practical steps, executives can strategically implement Generative AI solutions that offer personalized and efficient customer service, aligning with business objectives and customer expectations.

Step 1: Identifying Opportunities for AI Integration

Begin by conducting a thorough assessment of your current customer service channels and engagement points. Identify areas where customer interactions could be more efficient or personalized. For example, if your customer service team is overwhelmed with inquiries during peak hours, this could indicate an opportunity for AI to provide immediate responses. Similarly, if customers are seeking more personalized shopping experiences, Generative AI could be used to tailor product recommendations.

Practical Action: Map out the customer journey to pinpoint stages where customers seek information, make decisions, or require support. This will highlight key opportunities where AI can enhance the interaction.

Step 2: Selecting the Right AI Tools and Partners

With numerous Generative AI solutions available, it's essential to choose tools and partners that align with your specific needs and goals. Evaluate AI offerings not just on their technical capabilities, but also on how well they integrate with your existing systems and data infrastructure. Consider vendors that offer scalable solutions and demonstrate a clear understanding of your industry and customer base.

Practical Action: Create a checklist of criteria that AI solutions must meet, including ease of integration, scalability, data security, and compliance with regulations. Conduct pilot tests with shortlisted vendors to evaluate the effectiveness of their solutions in real-world scenarios.

Step 3: Implementing with a Customer-Centric Approach

When integrating AI into customer interactions, always prioritize the customer experience. Implementations should simplify and enhance the customer journey, not introduce additional complexity. Ensure that AI-driven interactions are seamless and intuitive, and that customers have the option to easily reach a human agent when needed. Incorporate fail-safes and human oversight to handle situations where the AI encounters queries beyond its capabilities or when customers express frustration or dissatisfaction.

Practical Action: Design the AI interaction flow to include clear options for customers to opt for human assistance at any point. Monitor AI–customer interactions closely in the initial stages to identify and rectify any friction points.

Step 4: Continuous Learning and Improvement

One of the strengths of Generative AI is its ability to learn and improve over time. Leverage this capability by continuously analyzing the outcomes of AI-driven interactions and identifying areas for enhancement. Collect and incorporate customer feedback to understand their experiences and expectations better. Use these insights to refine AI models, ensuring they remain aligned with customer needs and business goals.

Practical Action: Implement feedback mechanisms, such as post-interaction surveys or direct feedback options, to gather customer insights. Regularly review AI performance metrics and customer feedback data to identify trends and areas for improvement.

By following these steps, executives can successfully integrate Generative AI into their customer service and engagement strategies, creating a more personalized and efficient experience for their customers. Remember, the goal of implementing AI is to augment and enhance human capabilities, not to replace them. By combining the strengths of AI with the empathy and understanding of human agents, businesses can offer exceptional customer service that stands out in today's competitive landscape.

However, as you navigate the integration of Generative AI into customer service and engagement strategies, several challenges and considerations emerge. These range from ethical concerns regarding customer data to technical hurdles and organizational adjustments. Addressing these challenges head-on, with a focus on legal and ethical compliance, is essential for a successful and sustainable AI strategy.

Use of Customer Data

The use of customer data to train generative AI models raises significant privacy and ethical considerations. To navigate these responsibly, you must do the following:

> **Ensure Transparency**: Clearly inform customers about the data being collected and how it will be used. Transparency fosters trust and can alleviate concerns about data misuse.

> **Adopt Privacy by Design**: Integrate data protection and privacy considerations into the development and operation of AI systems from the outset.

> **Comply with Regulations**: Stay abreast of and comply with all relevant data protection laws and regulations, such as GDPR in Europe or CCPA in California, to ensure legal compliance and protect customer rights.

> **Practical Tip**: Implement regular audits of your AI systems and data usage practices to ensure ongoing compliance with privacy laws and ethical standards.

Overcoming Technical Integration Challenges with Existing Systems

Integrating Generative AI with legacy systems can be daunting due to compatibility and interoperability issues. To smooth this process, do the following:

Conduct a System Audit: Assess current IT infrastructure to identify potential integration challenges early.

Seek Modular Solutions: Opt for AI solutions that can be easily integrated into existing systems without extensive modifications.

Leverage APIs: Utilize application programming interfaces (APIs) to facilitate communication between the AI system and existing databases and applications.

Practical Tip: Engage with IT specialists and AI vendors who have experience in integrating AI with legacy systems to leverage their expertise and minimize disruptions.

Preparing for Organizational Changes, Including Staff Training and Shifts in Job Roles

The introduction of AI will inevitably lead to changes in job roles and the need for new skills. To manage this transition do the following:

Identify Skill Gaps: Assess the current skills of your workforce and identify gaps related to AI and data analysis.

Invest in Training: Provide training and upskilling opportunities to help employees adapt to new technologies and roles.

Foster a Culture of Adaptation: Encourage a culture that embraces change and innovation. Make it clear that AI is a tool to enhance, not replace, the human elements of customer service.

Practical Tip: Create a task force or assign a change manager to oversee the transition to AI-driven processes. This can help address concerns, manage resistance, and ensure a smooth adoption across the organization.

By proactively addressing these challenges and considerations, executives can ensure that the integration of Generative AI into customer interactions not only enhances operational efficiency and customer satisfaction but does so in a manner that is ethically responsible, legally compliant, and beneficial to both customers and employees. The key to success lies in balancing technological advancements with a commitment to ethical practices, privacy protection, and ongoing organizational adaptation.

The journey toward AI-enhanced interactions is not just a path to technological advancement but a stride toward redefining the customer experience. The transformative potential of Generative AI to elevate customer interactions through personalized and efficient service is immense, offering businesses an unparalleled opportunity to differentiate themselves in a competitive landscape.

A Call to Action

This journey to harness the full power of Generative AI begins with small, focused projects. These initial steps allow you to experiment with AI's capabilities, understand its impact on your operations, and gauge customer response to AI-driven interactions. Starting small affords you the agility to iterate and refine your approach based on real-world feedback, minimizing risks while maximizing the potential for meaningful insights.

Consider a pilot project that targets a specific aspect of your customer service—perhaps an AI-driven chatbot designed to handle frequently asked questions or a personalized recommendation engine for your online storefront. The key is to select a project that can provide quick wins, demonstrating the value of AI to both your customers and your organization.

As you glean insights and learnings from these initial endeavors, you'll be well positioned to scale AI initiatives across your organization. Each success story and lesson learned paves the way for broader implementation, informing strategies to further personalize customer interactions and streamline service processes. This iterative process of learning and scaling ensures that your AI integration efforts are continually refined, keeping pace with technological advancements and evolving customer expectations.

Conclusion

Generative AI in customer service and engagement heralds a new era of possibilities. This is the time for you to create your own vision of what is possible for your organization. By personalizing interactions in ways previously unimaginable and delivering services with unprecedented efficiency, your business stands to transform the very fabric of the customer experience. Of course, this journey requires thoughtful consideration, strategic planning, and an unwavering commitment to enhancing the human aspects of service with the intelligence and scalability of AI.

CHAPTER 5

Streamlining Operations with Generative AI

In today's fast-paced and competitive business landscape, executives are constantly seeking ways to optimize their operations and drive efficiency. Generative AI has emerged as a powerful tool for streamlining processes, automating tasks, and unlocking new insights. By leveraging the latest advancements in machine learning and natural language processing, organizations can transform their operations and gain a significant competitive advantage.

However, implementing Generative AI is not a simple plug-and-play solution. It requires careful planning, strategic execution, and ongoing management to realize its full potential. Executives must navigate a complex landscape of technology options, change-management challenges, and ethical considerations to successfully embed artificial intelligence (AI) into their operations.

In this chapter, we will explore the key strategies and best practices for streamlining operations through Generative AI. We will dive into the practical applications of AI across various operational areas, from supply chain management to customer service. We will also examine real-world case studies of organizations that have successfully leveraged AI

© Ahmed Bouzid, Paolo Narciso, Weiye Ma 2024
A. Bouzid et al., *Generative AI For Executives*,
https://doi.org/10.1007/979-8-8688-0950-7_5

to drive efficiency and innovation. By understanding the opportunities, challenges, and best practices for AI implementation, you can position your organization for success in the age of intelligent automation.

Identifying Opportunities for AI in Operations

To effectively harness Generative AI for operational efficiency, the initial step is a thorough process-mapping and AI-readiness assessment. This involves closely examining existing workflows to uncover inefficiencies, manual tasks, and bottlenecks where AI could add value through automation or augmentation. Executives should lead an AI-readiness assessment to evaluate the organization's data infrastructure, technology capabilities, and staff competencies, establishing the feasibility and potential scope for AI integration.

While Generative AI has a broad range of applications, organizations should prioritize areas where AI can deliver an immediate, significant impact. Key operational domains like supply chain management, inventory control, and customer service often see substantial benefits from using AI. For example, AI-driven demand forecasting can optimize inventory levels, while AI chatbots can handle routine customer inquiries, freeing human agents for complex issues. By targeting high-impact areas first, organizations can quickly demonstrate AI's value and drive momentum for broader adoption.

Process-Mapping and AI-Readiness Assessment

The first step in leveraging Generative AI to streamline operations is to thoroughly map out current processes and identify areas where AI can make an impact. This involves a detailed examination of each operational workflow, pinpointing bottlenecks, inefficiencies, and manual tasks that could be automated or augmented with AI. Executives should lead a comprehensive AI-readiness assessment, evaluating the organization's data infrastructure, technology capabilities, and staff skills to determine the feasibility and scope of AI integration.

Priority Areas for AI Integration

While the potential applications of Generative AI are vast, executives should prioritize operational areas where AI can deliver immediate and significant benefits. Supply chain management, inventory control, and customer service are often prime candidates. For example, AI-powered demand forecasting can optimize inventory levels, reducing carrying costs and stockouts. In customer service, AI chatbots can handle routine inquiries, freeing up human agents for more complex issues. By focusing on high-impact areas first, organizations can quickly demonstrate the value of AI and build momentum for broader adoption.

Generative AI Applications in Operations

Automated Content Generation

Generative AI excels at creating personalized content at scale, making it a valuable tool for marketing and customer communications. AI algorithms can analyze customer data, such as purchase history and preferences, to generate tailored email campaigns, product recommendations, and promotional offers. This not only saves time and resources but also enhances customer engagement and loyalty. Companies like Stitch Fix, an online personal styling service, use AI to generate personalized style suggestions and product descriptions for each customer, streamlining their styling process and improving customer satisfaction.

Predictive Maintenance and Operations

In manufacturing and service delivery environments, equipment downtime can be costly and disruptive. Generative AI models can analyze sensor data and maintenance records to predict when equipment is likely to fail, enabling proactive maintenance and minimizing unplanned outages. General Electric has implemented AI-powered predictive maintenance across its industrial equipment, from jet engines to wind turbines. By anticipating and addressing potential issues before they occur, GE has reduced maintenance costs and increased asset availability.

Dynamic Scheduling and Resource Allocation

Generative AI can optimize the scheduling of staff, resources, and logistics based on real-time data and predicted demand. In the healthcare industry, AI-driven scheduling systems can match patient needs with staff availability and expertise, improving resource utilization and patient outcomes. Qventus, an AI healthcare platform, uses machine learning to dynamically adjust hospital staffing levels and operating room schedules based on predicted patient volumes and acuity. This has led to significant reductions in wait times and increased operational efficiency.

Implementing Generative AI Solutions

To implement Generative AI solutions effectively, it's essential to align these technologies with your organization's existing IT infrastructure and strategic objectives. This process involves evaluating the current technology stack, choosing the right vendor, and strategically planning for initial deployments.

Technology Stack and Integration

Implementing Generative AI solutions requires careful consideration of the existing IT infrastructure and the necessary technology components. Executives should work closely with their technology teams to assess the current tech stack and identify any gaps or integration challenges. Key considerations include data storage and processing capabilities, network bandwidth, and security protocols. Cloud-based AI platforms, such as Google Cloud AI or Amazon Web Services, can provide scalable and flexible infrastructure for AI deployments.

Vendor Selection and Collaboration

Choosing the right AI technology vendor is critical for successful implementation. Executives should evaluate potential vendors based on their track record of successful deployments in similar industries, the robustness and scalability of their AI platforms, and their ability to provide ongoing support and training. It's also important to consider vendors' willingness to collaborate closely with the organization's internal teams to ensure smooth integration and knowledge transfer. IBM, for example, has partnered with numerous companies across industries to implement its Watson AI platform, providing tailored solutions and hands-on support.

Pilot Projects and Scaling

Before embarking on a full-scale AI implementation, it's prudent to start with pilot projects to demonstrate value and identify any challenges or limitations. Pilot projects should be focused on specific operational areas with clear performance metrics and success criteria. This allows organizations to test and refine their AI models in a controlled environment before scaling up. Once the pilot projects have proven successful, executives can develop a roadmap for wider AI rollout, prioritizing high-impact areas and ensuring the necessary resources and support are in place.

Training and Change Management

To successfully integrate Generative AI into operations, businesses need a well-prepared workforce and effective change-management strategies. Upskilling staff is crucial; executives must invest in training programs that focus on AI fundamentals, data analysis, and decision-making. This ensures that employees can effectively use AI tools, interpret outputs, and make informed decisions when unexpected or biased results occur. Companies like Airbus have pioneered internal AI academies to promote continuous learning and AI adoption.

Additionally, executives must lead AI implementation by clearly communicating its benefits and addressing concerns about job displacement. Highlighting how AI augments rather than replaces human skills can help build trust and engagement. To optimize AI use, organizations need robust feedback loops for continuous learning, ensuring AI models remain effective. Expanding AI applications over time by fostering a culture of innovation and experimentation can unlock new operational efficiencies and drive growth.

Upskilling Staff

Implementing Generative AI in operations requires a workforce that is equipped with the skills to work alongside AI tools and interpret their outputs. Executives should invest in comprehensive training and development programs to upskill staff in AI fundamentals, data analysis, and decision-making. This training should focus on how to use AI insights to make better operational decisions and when to intervene if the AI models produce unexpected or biased results. Companies like Airbus have launched internal AI academies to train employees across functions in AI skills, fostering a culture of continuous learning and AI adoption.

Change Leadership

Introducing AI into operations can be disruptive and may face resistance from staff who fear job displacement or loss of control. Executives must lead the change by communicating a clear vision for how AI will enhance operations and benefit employees. This includes highlighting how AI will augment rather than replace human capabilities, and how it will create new opportunities for growth and development. Leaders should actively engage staff in the AI implementation process, seeking their input and feedback and addressing any concerns transparently. By fostering a culture of experimentation and continuous improvement, executives can build buy-in and enthusiasm for AI-driven change.

Optimizing and Iterating AI Use
Feedback Loops and Continuous Learning

Generative AI models are not static; they require continuous refinement based on real-world performance and user feedback. Executives should establish clear feedback loops to capture data on AI model accuracy, user satisfaction, and operational impact. This feedback should be regularly analyzed to identify areas for improvement and inform updates to the AI algorithms. By embedding continuous learning into the AI implementation process, organizations can ensure that their AI tools remain relevant and effective over time.

Expanding AI Applications

As organizations gain experience and confidence with Generative AI, they can explore additional areas for AI integration beyond the initial use cases. This may involve applying AI to adjacent operational processes or exploring entirely new applications that emerge as the technology evolves. Executives should foster a culture of innovation and experimentation, encouraging teams to propose new AI ideas and providing the resources to test and scale promising initiatives. By continuously pushing the boundaries of AI use, organizations can stay ahead of the curve and unlock new sources of operational efficiency.

Case Studies and Best Practices

Generative AI has revolutionized operations across industries by delivering tangible results through innovative applications. Companies like Unilever and UPS have harnessed AI's power to enhance efficiency and cut costs. Unilever streamlined its hiring process by using AI to predict candidate success, slashing hiring time by 75% and significantly reducing expenses. UPS optimized delivery routes with AI, reducing fuel consumption and improving punctuality by continuously refining its algorithms based on real-time data. However, achieving success with AI requires careful navigation of challenges. Ensuring high-quality, unbiased data, managing realistic expectations, and addressing ethical concerns are essential for maximizing AI's potential while minimizing risks.

Success Stories

One powerful way to illustrate the potential of Generative AI in operations is through detailed case studies of successful implementations. Consider the example of Unilever, the global consumer goods company, which used AI to streamline its hiring process. By analyzing job descriptions, resumes, and candidate assessments, Unilever's AI system was able to predict job performance and cultural fit, reducing the time to hire by 75% and saving significant costs. Another example is UPS, the logistics giant, which used AI to optimize its delivery routes, reducing fuel consumption and improving on-time performance. By learning from driver feedback and real-time traffic data, UPS's AI system continuously refined its routing algorithms, leading to substantial operational efficiencies.

Lessons Learned and Pitfalls to Avoid

While the benefits of Generative AI are significant, executives must also be aware of common pitfalls and challenges. One key lesson is the importance of data quality and governance. AI models are only as good as the data they are trained on, so organizations must ensure that their data is accurate, complete, and free from bias. Another challenge is managing expectations around AI capabilities. While AI can automate many tasks, it is not a silver bullet and may require human oversight and intervention. Executives should set realistic goals for AI performance and be prepared to adjust their strategies based on real-world results. Finally, organizations must be vigilant about the ethical implications of AI use, such as potential job displacement or algorithmic bias, and develop clear guidelines and oversight mechanisms to mitigate these risks.

Evaluating AI Impact on Operations

To justify investment in Generative AI, executives must measure its impact on operations through metrics like cost savings, time reduction, and customer satisfaction while considering both direct benefits (e.g., reduced labor costs) and indirect benefits (e.g., improved morale). Beyond immediate gains, AI offers long-term advantages, such as greater agility, responsiveness, and strategic insights, creating a sustainable competitive edge.

Performance Metrics and ROI Analysis

To justify continued investment in Generative AI, executives must be able to quantify the impact on operations and demonstrate clear returns on investment (ROI). This requires establishing clear performance metrics and baselines before AI implementation, and regularly tracking progress against these metrics. Key indicators may include cost savings, time reductions, quality improvements, and customer satisfaction scores. ROI analysis should consider both the direct benefits of AI, such as reduced labor costs or increased output, as well as indirect benefits, such as improved employee morale or enhanced brand reputation.

Sustainability and Long-Term Benefits

While the immediate operational benefits of Generative AI are often the primary focus, executives should also consider the long-term strategic advantages. By embedding AI capabilities into their operations, organizations can become more agile, responsive, and data-driven. They can quickly adapt to changing market conditions, customer demands, and competitive pressures. Moreover, the insights generated by AI can inform strategic decision-making and help identify new growth opportunities. As AI becomes a core competency, organizations can develop a sustainable competitive advantage that is difficult for rivals to replicate.

Conclusion

Generative AI offers enormous potential to streamline operations and drive efficiency across industries. By carefully identifying opportunities, selecting the right applications, and managing the implementation process, executives can harness the power of AI to transform their organizations. However, success requires more than just technical capabilities; it demands a culture of continuous learning, experimentation, and adaptation. As AI technologies continue to evolve, the most successful organizations will be those that can effectively integrate AI into their operations while also nurturing the human skills and creativity that are essential for long-term growth and innovation.

CHAPTER 6

Harnessing Generative AI for Product Innovation

Because today's business landscape is rapidly evolving, staying ahead of the curve is not just an advantage—it's a necessity. As an executive in a small or medium-sized enterprise (SME), you're constantly seeking ways to innovate, differentiate, and capture new market opportunities. Generative artificial intelligence (AI) is a useful technology revolutionizing the way we approach product development and innovation.

Generative AI, which includes technologies like large language models (LLMs) and image generation tools, has the potential to transform every stage of the product development lifecycle. From ideation to market launch, this powerful technology can augment your team's capabilities, uncover hidden insights, and dramatically accelerate your innovation process.

In this chapter, we'll explore practical strategies for leveraging Generative AI to pioneer new products and services. We'll dive into real-world examples, provide actionable frameworks, and offer tips to help you integrate this technology into your product development workflow. By the end of this chapter, you'll be equipped with the knowledge and tools needed to harness the power of Generative AI and drive your company's innovation agenda forward.

© Ahmed Bouzid, Paolo Narciso, Weiye Ma 2024
A. Bouzid et al., *Generative AI For Executives*,
https://doi.org/10.1007/979-8-8688-0950-7_6

Generative AI in the Product Development Lifecycle

Let's examine how Generative AI can be applied at each stage of the product development lifecycle, including practical strategies for implementation.

Ideation and Market Research

Generative AI has the potential to supercharge your ideation process by synthesizing market trends, customer feedback, and competitive intelligence to generate novel product ideas. This technology can process vast amounts of data from diverse sources, identifying patterns and connections that might elude human analysts. By leveraging Generative AI in this phase, you can uncover hidden market opportunities, predict emerging trends, and generate innovative product concepts that align with evolving customer needs.

The power of Generative AI in ideation lies in its ability to combine and recombine ideas in novel ways, drawing from a vast knowledge base that spans industries and disciplines. It can help you break free from conventional thinking patterns and explore new possibilities that you might not have considered otherwise. Moreover, AI can rapidly iterate on ideas, generating hundreds of concepts in minutes, which your team can then evaluate and refine.

To implement this in practice, consider gathering a wide range of data sources, including customer reviews, social media posts, industry reports, and competitor information. This diverse dataset can then be fed into a Generative AI tool, such as a large language model. You can then prompt the AI with specific questions or challenges related to your product development goals. The key is to craft prompts that encourage the AI to think creatively and consider various angles of the problem.

For example, imagine you run a home appliance company. You might feed recent customer reviews, social media trends about home automation, and competitor product specs into a Generative AI tool. You could then prompt it with a question like: "Based on this data, what are some innovative smart home product ideas that could disrupt our industry?" The AI might suggest ideas such as a smart refrigerator that uses image recognition to track food inventory and automatically generates grocery lists, or an AI-powered thermostat that learns occupants' schedules and preferences to optimize energy usage.

It's important to remember that while Generative AI can produce a wealth of ideas, the role of human creativity and expertise remains crucial. Use the AI-generated ideas as a starting point for further exploration and refinement by your product team. Encourage your team to build upon these ideas, combining them with their own insights and industry knowledge to create truly innovative product concepts.

User Research and Persona Development

Generative AI can significantly enhance your user research efforts and help create more detailed, nuanced user personas. This technology can analyze vast amounts of user data, including demographic information, behavioral patterns, and even unstructured data like social media posts or customer service interactions. By processing this diverse dataset, Generative AI can identify patterns and segments that might not be immediately apparent to human researchers.

One of the key advantages of using Generative AI in persona development is its ability to create more dynamic, multidimensional personas. Traditional persona development often results in static, oversimplified representations of user groups. In contrast, AI-enhanced personas can incorporate a wider range of variables and can be updated in real-time as new data becomes available. This leads to a more accurate and nuanced understanding of your target users, which in turn informs better product design decisions.

Moreover, Generative AI can simulate user behavior and generate potential user scenarios. This capability allows you to explore how different user types might interact with your product in various contexts, helping you identify potential pain points or opportunities for improvement before you even begin prototyping.

To implement this strategy, start by gathering a comprehensive dataset about your users. This could include demographic data, user surveys, behavioral analytics from your existing products or similar products in the market, and even relevant social media data. Feed this data into a Generative AI tool, such as a large language model, and prompt it to create detailed user personas based on this information.

For instance, if you're developing a fitness app, you might prompt the AI to create distinct user personas and describe their typical week of app usage. The AI could generate personas like Sarah, a 28-year-old busy professional who uses the app for quick morning yoga and weekend runs; Michael, a 45-year-old health-conscious parent who uses the app for strength training and family activities; and Emma, a 60-year-old retiree focusing on wellness through low-impact exercises and meditation.

These AI-generated personas provide a starting point for understanding diverse user needs and behaviors. However, it's crucial to validate and refine these personas through real-world user research. Use the AI-generated personas as a basis for discussion with your team and actual users. This combination of AI-driven insights and human validation can lead to a more comprehensive and accurate understanding of your target audience.

Remember, the goal is not to replace traditional user research methods, but to augment them. Generative AI can help you cast a wider net, identify patterns you might have missed, and generate hypotheses for further investigation. It can also help you rapidly iterate on your personas as you gather more data and insights throughout the product development process.

Product Design and Prototyping

Generative AI is revolutionizing the product design and prototyping phase by enabling rapid iteration, exploring a wider range of design possibilities, and even assisting in the creation of functional prototypes. This technology can significantly speed up the design process while also encouraging more innovative and user-centric design solutions.

In the realm of visual design, AI image generation tools can create multiple design concepts based on specified requirements and constraints. These tools can produce a variety of visual elements, from UI components to complete interface layouts, providing designers with a rich source of inspiration and a starting point for further refinement. The ability to quickly generate and iterate on design concepts allows teams to explore a much broader range of possibilities than traditional methods would allow.

Beyond visual design, Generative AI is also making strides in functional design and prototyping. AI-powered tools can assist in creating interactive prototypes, generating basic code structures, and even suggesting optimal user flows based on established design patterns and user behavior data. This capability is particularly valuable for digital products, where rapid prototyping can significantly accelerate the development cycle.

To implement AI-assisted design and prototyping in your product development process, start by clearly defining your product requirements and design constraints. These could include factors like target user demographics, key functionalities, brand guidelines, and any technical limitations. Use these parameters to guide your interactions with the AI design tools.

For example, if you're designing a new smart-home control panel, you might start by prompting an AI image generation tool to create a sleek, minimalist design for a wall-mounted panel with a 7-inch touchscreen. Once you have initial designs, you can use natural language prompts to modify and refine these designs. You might ask the AI to add a voice control button to the top right corner, change the color scheme to cool blues and greys, or show how the interface would look when controlling lighting.

For prototyping, you could then use an AI coding assistant to create a basic HTML and CSS prototype based on the chosen design. This rapid prototyping capability allows you to quickly move from concept to a tangible, interactive model that can be used for user testing and stakeholder presentations.

It's important to note that while AI can greatly accelerate the design and prototyping process, human creativity and expertise remain crucial. AI-generated designs should always be reviewed and refined by experienced designers who can ensure that the final product aligns with user needs, brand identity, and design best practices. The AI is a tool to speed up the process and generate ideas, not a replacement for human creativity and user-centric design principles.

Moreover, AI can be particularly valuable in the iterative design process. As you gather feedback on initial designs and prototypes, you can feed this information back into the AI system to generate refined versions. This creates a powerful feedback loop that combines user insights, designer expertise, and AI capabilities to rapidly evolve and improve the product design.

Product Development and Testing

While the core development work will still be done by your engineering team, Generative AI can significantly enhance various aspects of the product development and testing process. By leveraging AI in this phase, you can potentially reduce development time, improve code quality, and catch potential issues earlier in the development cycle.

One of the primary ways Generative AI is assisting in product development is through advanced code generation and optimization. AI coding assistants can generate boilerplate code, suggest optimizations, and even help solve complex algorithmic problems. These tools are becoming increasingly sophisticated, capable of understanding context and producing code that adheres to best practices and your specific coding standards.

However, it's crucial to understand that AI-generated code is not meant to replace human developers. Instead, it serves as a productivity tool, allowing developers to focus on more complex, creative aspects of software development. Human oversight remains essential to ensure that the generated code aligns with the overall architecture and meets all functional requirements.

In addition to code generation, Generative AI can be a powerful ally in creating and maintaining technical documentation. AI can analyze your codebase and generate clear, comprehensive documentation, including function descriptions, API references, and even usage examples. This can significantly reduce the time developers spend on documentation, ensuring that it remains up-to-date as the product evolves.

Testing is another area where Generative AI can provide substantial benefits. AI can generate comprehensive test cases, including edge cases that human testers might overlook. By analyzing the structure and behavior of your software, AI can identify potential weak points and create tests to probe these areas thoroughly. This capability is particularly valuable for complex systems where manual creation of exhaustive test suites would be time-consuming and prone to oversights.

Furthermore, AI-powered code-review tools can be implemented to catch potential bugs early in the development process. These tools can analyze code for security vulnerabilities, performance issues, and adherence to coding standards, providing developers with immediate feedback and suggestions for improvement.

To implement these AI-enhanced development and testing strategies, consider integrating AI coding assistants into your development environment. Train your team on how to effectively use these tools, emphasizing that they are aids to augment their skills, not replace them. Implement AI-powered code review as part of your continuous integration pipeline to catch issues early and consistently.

For example, during the development of a smart-home app, you might use AI in several ways. You could prompt an AI coding assistant to generate a Python function to efficiently schedule and optimize energy usage across multiple smart-home devices. For documentation, you might ask the AI to create user-friendly documentation for the API endpoints of your smart-home control system. In testing, you could have the AI generate a list of test cases for your smart thermostat function, including edge cases like power outages and extreme temperature changes.

While AI can greatly assist in development and testing, it's crucial to have experienced developers oversee the process. AI-generated code should always be reviewed and tested thoroughly by your team. The goal is to use AI as a tool to enhance productivity and quality, not as a replacement for human expertise and judgment.

Marketing and Launch

Generative AI is transforming the marketing landscape, offering powerful tools for content creation, personalization, and strategic planning. By leveraging AI in your marketing and launch efforts, you can create more engaging content, deliver personalized experiences at scale, and optimize your launch strategies based on data-driven insights.

One of the key applications of Generative AI in marketing is content creation. AI can analyze your brand voice from existing marketing materials and generate new content that aligns with your brand identity. This capability extends across various content types, including marketing copy, social media posts, email campaigns, and even basic video scripts.

The ability to rapidly generate high-quality, on-brand content can significantly accelerate your marketing efforts and ensure consistency across channels.

However, it's important to keep in mind that while AI can generate a large volume of content quickly, human oversight remains crucial. Marketing teams should review and refine AI-generated content to ensure it truly captures the nuances of your brand voice and meets your quality standards. Think of AI as a collaborative partner in the creative process, providing ideas and drafts that human marketers can then polish and perfect.

Personalization is another area where Generative AI excels. By analyzing customer data and behavior patterns, AI can help create highly personalized marketing messages for different customer segments. This level of personalization, which would be time-consuming and challenging to achieve manually at scale, can significantly improve engagement rates and conversion.

In terms of launch planning, Generative AI can analyze data from past product launches (both yours and those of competitors) to suggest optimal launch strategies. It can help identify the most-effective channels, timing, and messaging for your specific product and target audience. This data-driven approach can help you make more-informed decisions and potentially improve the success rate of your product launches.

To implement AI-powered marketing and launch strategies, start by feeding your existing marketing materials into an AI system to analyze and understand your brand voice. You can then use this AI model to generate marketing copy, social media posts, and other content. For personalization, leverage your customer data to create distinct segments, and use AI to generate tailored messages for each segment.

For example, when launching a new smart-home system, you might use AI to analyze your previous product descriptions and identify key phrases and tones that define your brand voice. You could then ask the AI to write a series of social media posts announcing the new system, emphasizing key features like energy efficiency and user-friendly design. For personalization, you might have the AI create multiple versions of your product announcement email, each tailored to a specific customer segment, such as tech enthusiasts, busy professionals, or eco-conscious consumers.

When it comes to launch planning, you could prompt the AI to analyze data from your previous launches and industry trends, and then suggest an optimal timeline and channel mix for your smart-home system launch. This might include recommendations on which social media platforms to prioritize, the best time to send email announcements, or ideas for launch events or promotions.

Remember, while AI can provide valuable insights and automate many aspects of marketing and launch planning, human creativity and strategic thinking remain essential. Use AI-generated ideas and content as a starting point, but always apply your own expertise and understanding of your specific market and customers to refine and optimize your marketing and launch strategies.

Framework: The AI-Augmented Innovation Cycle

To help you integrate Generative AI into your product development process, consider the following framework: The AI-Augmented Innovation Cycle. This framework provides a structured approach to leveraging AI throughout the product development lifecycle, ensuring that you're maximizing the potential of this technology at every stage.

The cycle begins with Insight Generation. In this phase, Generative AI is used to analyze market data, customer feedback, and trends. By processing vast amounts of information from diverse sources, AI can identify patterns and connections that might not be immediately apparent to human analysts. The AI can then generate potential product ideas and innovations based on these insights. This phase is about casting a wide net and exploring possibilities, with AI acting as a creative partner in the ideation process.

Next comes Concept Development. Here, AI is leveraged to create detailed user personas and scenarios. By analyzing user data and behavior patterns, AI can help build more nuanced, dynamic personas that reflect the complexity of your target audience. Additionally, AI-assisted design tools can be used to visualize product concepts quickly. This rapid visualization capability allows you to explore a wider range of design possibilities in a shorter time frame.

The third phase is Prototype Creation. In this stage, AI coding assistants can be employed to rapidly create basic prototypes. This is particularly useful for digital products, where AI can generate functional code based on design specifications. AI can also be used to generate comprehensive test cases and simulate user interactions, providing early insights into how users might engage with the product.

Following prototype creation is the Validation and Refinement phase. Here, AI can be used to analyze user feedback simulations and suggest iterative improvements based on validation results. This creates a rapid feedback loop, allowing you to quickly refine your product based on simulated user interactions and potential real-world scenarios.

The fifth phase is Launch Preparation. In this stage, AI is utilized for marketing content creation and personalization. By understanding your brand voice and target audience, AI can generate marketing materials that resonate with your customers. AI can also be employed to optimize launch strategies and timelines, analyzing past launch data to suggest the most effective approach.

The final phase, which feeds back into the beginning of the cycle, is Continuous Improvement. Here, AI is leveraged to constantly analyze post-launch data and generate ongoing product improvement suggestions. This ensures that your product continues to evolve and improve based on real-world usage and changing market conditions.

This cycle is iterative, with insights from each stage feeding back into the others. The key is to view AI as a collaborative tool that augments human creativity and decision-making at each stage. By following this framework, you can ensure that you're leveraging the power of Generative AI throughout your product development process, from initial idea to post-launch improvements.

It's important to note that while this framework provides a structured approach to integrating AI into your product development process, it should be adapted to fit your specific organizational needs and product types. The goal is not to rigidly follow a prescribed process, but to thoughtfully incorporate AI in ways that enhance your existing workflows and drive innovation.

Overcoming Challenges and Ethical Considerations

While Generative AI offers immense potential for product innovation, it's crucial to be aware of and address potential challenges and ethical considerations. As an executive, it's your responsibility to ensure that your organization's use of AI is not only effective but also ethical and responsible.

Data privacy is a primary concern when working with AI systems. These technologies often require large amounts of data to function effectively, which can include sensitive customer information. It's crucial to ensure that any data fed into AI systems complies with privacy regulations such as GDPR or CCPA, as well as your company's own data policies. Implement robust data protection measures, including data anonymization and encryption, and be transparent with your customers about how their data is being used.

Bias in AI systems is another significant challenge. AI models can perpetuate or even amplify biases present in their training data. This could lead to product designs or marketing strategies that inadvertently discriminate against certain groups. To mitigate this risk, it's essential to have diverse human oversight throughout the AI-augmented product development process. Regularly audit your AI outputs for potential biases and take corrective action when necessary. Consider forming a diverse AI ethics committee within your organization to provide ongoing guidance and oversight.

There's also a risk of over-reliance on AI systems. While Generative AI is a powerful tool, it should not replace human judgment and creativity. It's crucial to maintain a balance, using AI to augment human capabilities rather than replace them. Encourage your team to view AI as a collaborative partner, not an infallible oracle. Foster an environment where team members feel comfortable questioning and critically evaluating AI-generated outputs.

Intellectual property concerns can arise when using Generative AI in product development. The legal landscape around AI-generated content and inventions is still evolving, and it's not always clear who owns the rights to AI-generated ideas or designs. Consult with legal experts to navigate this complex area and establish clear policies around the ownership and use of AI-generated intellectual property within your organization.

Ethical use of AI extends beyond your immediate product development process. Consider the broader societal impacts of your AI-enhanced products. Will they contribute positively to society? Could they potentially be misused or have unintended negative consequences? These are crucial questions to address as part of your product development process.

To address these challenges effectively, consider implementing the following strategies:

1. Develop clear AI ethics guidelines for your organization. These should cover data usage, bias mitigation, intellectual property, and broader ethical considerations.

2. Provide comprehensive training to your team on AI capabilities, limitations, and ethical considerations. This will help them use AI tools more effectively and responsibly.

3. Implement a system of checks and balances in your AI-augmented product development process. This could include regular audits of AI outputs, diverse review panels, and/or mechanisms for employees to raise ethical concerns.

4. Stay informed about evolving AI regulations and best practices. The AI landscape is rapidly changing, and it's crucial to keep your policies and practices up-to-date.

5. Be transparent with your customers about your use of AI in product development and how it benefits them. This can help build trust and differentiate your brand.

By proactively addressing these challenges and ethical considerations, you can harness the power of Generative AI while maintaining the trust of your customers and contributing positively to society.

Getting Started: Practical Next Steps

Embarking on your Generative AI journey in product development requires careful planning and a strategic approach. Let's look at some practical steps to get you started.

Begin by assessing your organization's AI readiness. This involves evaluating your current data infrastructure, team capabilities, and potential use cases for Generative AI. Consider factors such as the quality and quantity of your data, the technical skills of your team, and the specific areas of your product development process that could benefit most from AI augmentation. This assessment will help you identify your starting point and prioritize your AI initiatives.

Once you've completed your assessment, start small with a pilot project. Choose one area of your product development process, such as ideation or market research, where you believe Generative AI could have a significant impact. This allows you to experiment with AI in a controlled environment, learn from the experience, and demonstrate value before scaling up. For example, you might start by using a Generative AI tool to analyze customer feedback and generate product improvement ideas for an existing product line.

Investing in learning is crucial for successful AI implementation. Provide training for your team on AI fundamentals, including how to effectively prompt and interact with AI tools. This training should cover not just the technical aspects of AI but also the ethical considerations and best practices for responsible AI use. Consider partnering with AI experts or educational institutions to develop a comprehensive training program tailored to your organization's needs.

Choosing the right tools is another critical step. Research and select Generative AI tools that align with your specific needs and integrate well with your existing workflows. There are numerous AI platforms and tools available, ranging from general-purpose language models to specialized tools for design, coding, or market analysis. Take the time to evaluate different options, considering factors such as ease of use, customization capabilities, and alignment with your data privacy requirements.

As you implement AI in your product development process, it's essential to measure and iterate. Set clear Key Performance Indicators (KPIs) for your AI initiatives. These might include metrics such as time saved in the ideation process, increase in the number of product concepts generated, or improvement in customer satisfaction with new products. Continuously measure the impact of your AI initiatives against these KPIs and be prepared to adjust your approach based on the results.

Fostering a culture of innovation is crucial for successful AI adoption. Encourage your team to experiment with AI and share learnings across the organization. Create channels for knowledge sharing, such as regular AI showcase sessions where team members can present their experiences and insights from using AI in their work. Celebrate successes and learn from setbacks, viewing them all as valuable steps in your AI journey.

Consider creating an AI Center of Excellence within your organization. This cross-functional team can serve as internal AI experts, providing guidance, sharing best practices, and helping to scale AI usage across different departments. They can also stay abreast of the latest developments in AI technology and ensure that your organization is leveraging cutting-edge capabilities.

Finally, don't forget the importance of change management. Introducing AI into your product development process represents a significant change, and it's crucial to manage this transition carefully. Communicate clearly with your team about the role of AI, addressing any concerns or misconceptions. Emphasize that AI is a tool to augment their capabilities, not replace them. Involve key stakeholders in the AI implementation process to ensure buy-in and smooth adoption.

By following these steps, you can begin to harness the power of Generative AI in your product development process. Remember, the goal is not to replace human creativity and expertise, but to augment it, enabling your team to innovate faster and more effectively than ever before.

Conclusion

Generative AI represents a paradigm shift in product innovation, offering SMEs the power to compete with larger enterprises by dramatically enhancing their ability to generate ideas, understand users, and bring products to market faster. By thoughtfully integrating AI into your product development process, you can unlock new levels of creativity, efficiency, and market responsiveness.

As you embark on this journey, it's crucial to maintain a balance between leveraging AI capabilities and preserving human creativity and judgment. The most successful implementations of Generative AI in product development will be those that effectively combine the analytical power and scalability of AI with human ingenuity, domain expertise, and ethical considerations.

Remember that adopting Generative AI is not just about implementing new tools—it's about embracing a new way of thinking about product development. It requires a willingness to experiment, learn, and sometimes fail. Encourage your team to be curious, to push the boundaries of what's possible, and to always keep the needs of your users at the forefront.

As you move forward, stay informed about the rapidly evolving AI landscape. New capabilities and best practices are emerging all the time, and staying up-to-date will help you maintain a competitive edge. At the same time, remain vigilant about the ethical implications of AI use, ensuring that your AI-enhanced products contribute positively to society.

The future of product innovation is here, and with Generative AI, you have the tools to shape it. Your next groundbreaking product idea could be just a prompt away. Are you ready to pioneer the future? The journey may be challenging, but the potential rewards—in terms of innovation, efficiency, and competitive advantage—are immense. Embrace the power of Generative AI, and let it propel your product development to new heights.

CHAPTER 7

Strategies for Successful Generative AI Implementation

By now, it should be obvious that Generative AI represents a transformative technology that has the potential to revolutionize (and is already revolutionizing) industries by enhancing creativity, facilitating if not completely automating complex tasks, eliminating costly points of failure, and driving overall organizational efficiency.

For business-oriented, non-technical executives, navigating the complexities of integrating Generative AI can be daunting, to say the least.

In this chapter, we provide a guide to implementing Generative AI within your organization, covering the assessment of organizational readiness, developing a clear artificial intelligence (AI) strategy, investing in the necessary technology infrastructure, and building a skilled workforce.

Additionally, we highlight the necessity of fostering a culture of innovation, ensuring ethical AI use, and measuring implementation success.

Real-world case studies offer practical insights and lessons, equipping executives with the tools needed to harness Generative AI for achieving strategic business goals, driving competitive advantage, and promoting innovation as the self-perpetuating loop in which greater implementation can propel business ever higher.

© Ahmed Bouzid, Paolo Narciso, Weiye Ma 2024
A. Bouzid et al., *Generative AI For Executives*,
https://doi.org/10.1007/979-8-8688-0950-7_7

Assessing Organizational Readiness

A successful implementation of Generative AI needs to begin with an accurate mapping of where your organization currently stands on a number of key points.

Both industry analysis as well as multiple use cases demonstrate that there is an obvious, legitimate, and pronounced benefit to business at large waiting within Generative AI; its ability to facilitate and enhance business processes is huge.

Going forward, what will separate the success stories from the rest will be a preliminary analysis that determines the correct point of departure for Generative AI implementation.

Such an analysis will touch on a number of key points that will highlight your organization's preparedness, as well as pinpoint the speed and nature of derived benefits post-implementation.

Current Technology Landscape: Evaluating Existing Infrastructure

Before diving into Generative AI, it's crucial to understand your organization's current technological capabilities. This involves evaluating existing IT infrastructure, data management systems, and software tools.

Key considerations will include the following:

> **Infrastructure assessment**. You'll need a review of your current hardware and software to determine if they can support AI workloads—Generative AI models often require substantial computational power, including GPUs or TPUs.

> **Data infrastructure**. You'll need to assess your data collection, storage, and processing capabilities. High-quality data in large volumes are essential

to effectively train AI models—just as a varied and nutrient-rich diet builds healthy organisms, so too does well-ordered, comprehensive, and substantial data build truly useful AI.

Software ecosystem. Focusing specifically on software, you'll also have to evaluate your existing software and platforms to determine compatibility with Generative AI tools. Integration with existing systems can impact the efficiency (and ultimate effectiveness) of implementation, and it's important to provide the appropriate arena in which Generative AI can do its best work, unhindered by compatibility issues.

AI Maturity Assessment: Determining the Organization's Readiness for AI Integration

"AI maturity" refers to your organization's readiness to adopt and integrate AI technologies—internal issues of resistance due to disinterest, intimidation, or misunderstanding will devalue Generative AI's benefit to business.

This assessment will involve the following:

Current AI use. You'll want to determine if and how your organization already uses AI in any capacity—something not necessarily always obvious and known to executives. Even peripheral experience with AI can ease the transition to more advanced Generative AI systems.

Strategic alignment. You'll also want to evaluate how AI aligns with your current business goals. Pointedly, organizations with a strategic focus on digital transformation are more likely to succeed in AI integration in every way that counts.

Organizational culture. Finally, assess whether your organizational culture supports technological change—a slightly different kettle of fish* than digital transformation. A culture that embraces innovation and change is better suited for AI adoption and will derive the full benefits of Generative AI..

Gap Analysis: Identifying Gaps in Technology, Skills, and Processes

Conducting a gap analysis will help you to identify potential discrepancies between your current organizational capabilities and those required for successful AI implementation.

When doing the analysis, it helps to delineate three broad areas of focus, as follows:

1. **Technology gaps.** You'll identify any deficiencies in hardware, software, or data infrastructure that need to be addressed.

2. **Skills gaps**. Likewise, you have to assess the existing skill sets within the organization and identify gaps in AI-related knowledge and expertise.

3. **Process gaps**. You also need to evaluate your current processes and workflows so as to determine how they need to adapt to integrate AI effectively.

108

Developing a Clear AI Strategy

Developing your organizational demands of Generative AI does presume an at least superficial understanding of its capabilities, but a strategic approach to its implementation is essential.

Studies show that those who embark upon proactive AI implementation with their organizational goals and strategic deployment ideas firmly in hand enjoy the greatest success.

Vision and Goals: Defining the Vision for AI within your Organization

A clear AI strategy begins with a well-defined vision, as follows:

> **Strategic vision**. Your strategic vision should articulate how Generative AI aligns with the organization's overall strategic goals. This vision should outline how AI will create value and drive business success. A more detailed vision than a mere outline is preferable, based on organizational history and current realities, as it will give you defined goals to pursue in implementation.

> **Objectives**. Set specific, measurable, achievable, relevant, and time-bound (SMART) objectives for AI implementation. These objectives should guide the development and deployment of AI solutions if Generative AI is to enable your organization to achieve its broader goals.

Use Case Identification: Selecting High-Impact, Feasible Use Cases for Generative AI

Identifying relevant use cases is crucial for deriving maximum benefit from Generative AI.

It's a good idea to include some use cases that might be less technically challenging, but provide rapid results, as this provides traction for a positive implementation ethos by providing a tangible demonstration for those still intimidated or otherwise on the strategic periphery.

> **High-impact use cases**. Choose use cases that address critical business challenges or opportunities. Prioritize areas where Generative AI can deliver significant value, such as customer personalization, content creation, or process automation.

> **Feasibility assessment**. You'll also need to evaluate the technical feasibility and resource requirements of each use case to ensure that chosen use cases align with available technology and your organizational capabilities.

Roadmap Creation: Establishing a Phased Implementation Plan

As with many other aspects of business, developing a roadmap ensures a structured approach to AI implementation.

Begin your implementation with pilot projects that can test AI solutions on a smaller scale before looking to do a full-scale deployment. Once you have completed your pilot projects, you can then use the insights gained from those projects to refine your strategies and address any challenges that may have surfaced.

110

The benefits of roadmapping implementation will include the following:

Strategic alignment. A roadmap helps to keep Generative AI initiatives aligned with your organization's overall strategic goals. It ensures that the implementation of Generative AI is driven by a clear vision and purpose, enabling the organization to focus on high-impact areas (*and* avoid unnecessary detours).

Prioritization and resource allocation efficiencies. A roadmap also allows your organization to prioritize Generative AI projects based on feasibility, potential impact, and alignment with strategic priorities. It helps you allocate resources effectively, including budget, personnel, and infrastructure, ensuring that projects receive the necessary support.

Phased implementation. Developing a roadmap will also enable your organization to plan and execute Generative AI implementation in a *phased manner*, allowing for incremental progress, reducing risks, and providing opportunities for learning and adjustment along the way. It also helps manage expectations and build momentum within the organization. It should include short-term and long-term goals, as well as outline key milestones, timelines, and resource allocation.

Risk mitigation. A roadmap will be an aid in identifying possible challenges and risks that Generative AI implementation could foment. By considering factors such as data privacy, security,

111

ethical considerations, and regulatory compliance, you can proactively address these issues and develop appropriate mitigation strategies.

Performance measurement. Furthermore, a roadmap provides a framework for measuring the progress and success of your Generative AI initiatives. It helps define key performance indicators (KPIs) specific to each project, enabling you to track and evaluate the impact of Generative AI on your business outcomes. Real-time monitoring and performance measurement are the ensuing components that allow for timely adjustments and course corrections.

Change management and stakeholder engagement. Developing a roadmap will involve engaging with stakeholders from multiple departments and various levels of your organization. Such engagement fosters a sense of ownership and collaboration, ensuring that Generative AI initiatives are embraced and supported throughout the organization. It also facilitates effective change management by addressing concerns, providing training, and (importantly) communicating the benefits of Generative AI.

Long-term vision and adaptability. A roadmap provides a long-term vision for Generative AI implementation, considering both your current and future needs. It allows your organization to adapt and evolve its Generative AI strategy as technology advances, business requirements change, and new opportunities emerge. Regular reviews and updates to the roadmap ensure that you'll stay on track and can effectively respond to new developments.

Investing in Technology Infrastructure

Investing in technology infrastructure is crucial for organizations looking to implement Generative AI effectively. It involves three core areas: data management, AI tools and platforms, and integration with existing systems. Each of these areas plays a vital role in ensuring that Generative AI solutions are not only functional but also optimized for business needs, as follows:

> **Data management** is foundational for AI, requiring robust systems for data collection, storage, and processing. High-quality data collection ensures AI models receive accurate, unbiased input. Secure and scalable storage, often cloud-based, is necessary to handle large datasets, while efficient processing pipelines prepare data for model training.

> **AI tools and platforms** are the backbone of Generative AI implementation. Selecting the right AI tools and platforms that align with organizational goals and technical capabilities is essential. This involves evaluating the scalability, usability, and integration capabilities of various AI platforms and tools to ensure they fit the organization's needs.

113

Integration with existing systems is the final piece of the puzzle. Smooth integration with current IT infrastructure requires meticulous planning, thorough testing, and validation to avoid disruptions. A well-thought-out integration strategy ensures that AI solutions are seamlessly assimilated, maximizing their potential and minimizing risks.

Investing in these areas helps organizations create a solid foundation for deploying generative AI, driving innovation, and achieving long-term success.

Data Management: Ensuring Robust Data Collection, Storage, and Processing Capabilities

Effective data management is essential for the success of Generative AI; in a real sense, they're the two ends of the same stick.

All of the best preparation in the world won't salvage implementation if an organization is haphazard in its data management.

Astute data management that will aid Generative AI includes the following:

Data collection. You need to have robust data collection mechanisms to gather high-quality data from all relevant sources, ensuring that data is representative of the problems to be solved and that it remains free from biases.

Data storage. If you're looking at implementing AI solutions, you should be investing in scalable and secure data storage solutions. Cloud-based storage options can very often provide the right amount of flexibility needed to handle large volumes of data.

Data processing. You'll want to develop efficient data processing pipelines to clean, pre-process, and manage data (while ensuring that your data processing capabilities can support the demands of AI model training).

AI Tools and Platforms: Selecting Appropriate AI Platforms and Tools

Choosing the right AI tools and platforms is critical for effective implementation—here, one size does not fit all.

This consideration will require a fair amount of research, but implementation pays dividends to those who take the time to do the following homework:

AI platforms. Evaluate AI platforms that offer the necessary capabilities for building and deploying Generative AI models, considering factors likes scalability, ease of use, *and* integration capabilities.

Tool selection. You want to select tools that align with your organization's needs and expertise (consider tools for model training, deployment, and monitoring).

Integration with Existing Systems: Strategies for Smooth Integration with Your Current IT

Integrating Generative AI with existing systems requires careful planning, but it's another arena where those who are prepared to map it out carefully are eligible for the greatest rewards (ease of assimilation with minimal hiccups).

115

Here, casting the net wide for input pays dividends, as you'll want all valid input, and a single observation can illuminate a potential pitfall to be eliminated. See the following:

> **Integration plan**. You need to develop a detailed integration plan that outlines how AI solutions will interface with current IT systems, clearly addressing potential challenges and dependencies.

> **Testing and validation**. You should also conduct thorough testing to ensure that AI integrations work seamlessly with existing systems, validating performance and reliability before full deployment.

Building a Skilled Workforce

To successfully implement AI, building a skilled workforce is critical, focusing on the people who will make AI projects succeed. This involves hiring experts, upskilling current employees, and forming teams that blend technical and business expertise.

> **Talent acquisition: Hiring AI experts and data scientists**. Recruitment should focus on identifying AI specialists, data scientists, and machine learning engineers with the right skills and experience. Look for candidates with a deep understanding of AI, proven domain expertise, and a portfolio that demonstrates their abilities. Assess their skills to ensure they fit your organization's needs, minimizing the need for extensive training and aligning them with your implementation goals from day one.

Training and development: Upskilling existing employees. Upskilling current employees is essential to maximize AI's potential in your business. Develop training programs to enhance their understanding of AI technologies and foster continuous learning. Promote knowledge sharing and collaboration to create a learning environment where employees can exchange insights and accelerate their expertise, leading to faster and more confident AI deployment.

Cross-functional teams: Blending technical and business expertise. Form cross-functional teams that combine technical experts with business professionals to ensure AI solutions are both technically sound and aligned with business goals. A diverse team enhances problem-solving, drives innovation, and ensures AI tools are practical and effective for your organization's needs. Encourage meaningful collaboration to bridge gaps between technical and business perspectives, creating AI solutions that truly support your business objectives.

Talent Acquisition: Hiring AI Experts and Data Scientists

Building a skilled workforce is essential for AI implementation to become a success (the people factor).

Generative AI specialists will have a crisp understanding of how to go about things, and also (crucially) be able to pinpoint limits and redirect when things need to be done a different way. See the following:

> **Talent recruitment**. Identify and recruit AI experts, data scientists, and machine learning engineers with the necessary skills and experience. Look for candidates with a strong background in AI and relevant domain expertise. Good candidates will speak a language you understand and have a great portfolio of expertise.

> **Skills assessment**. Evaluate the skills and qualifications of potential hires to ensure they meet your organization's needs, considering candidates with experience in Generative AI and related technologies (a good fit is crucial, to eliminate having to manage both their learning curve as well as your organization's aims in implementation—it's unnecessary).

Training and Development: Upskilling Existing Employees on AI Technologies and Practices

Upskilling existing employees is crucial for maximizing the value of the AI you seek to implement as a business aid, and should follow the format of conventional upskilling as follows:

> **Training programs**. Develop and implement training programs to enhance employees' understanding of AI technologies and practices, and provide resources and support for continuous learning.

Knowledge sharing. In implementation, encourage knowledge sharing and collaboration among employees to foster a learning environment where employees can exchange insights and experiences related to AI. A communal pool of new experiences leads to quicker confidence and smoother end results.

Cross-Functional Teams: Creating Teams with a Mix of Technical and Business Expertise

Cross-functional teams can bridge the gap between technical and business perspectives, as they often do in legacy business, and the model finds perfect application in corporate implementation of AI.

Diversity here is essential so that outcomes don't lean toward technical exclusivity, nor get watered down by less technical voices to become substandard tools.

Basic but essential considerations here include the following:

Team composition. Create teams that include a mix of technical experts and business professionals, as such diversity enhances problem-solving and innovation (implementing Generative AI is a wholly innovative space).

Collaboration. A tired and overused term, but collaboration needs to be promoted to generate definite participation between technical and business teams to ensure that AI solutions aid and align with business objectives and requirements.

Fostering a Culture of Innovation

While "a culture of innovation" has become a catchy byline for all and sundry in business, it remains essential in the modern marketplace.

For those who genuinely grasp its significance, it boils down to some fairly basic imperatives that start at the top.

Leadership Commitment

Gaining buy-in from top management is the first order of business, as leadership commitment is essential for driving successful AI adoption.

The following considerations prevail here:

> **Executive support**. You'll want to secure support from top management to ensure that AI initiatives receive the necessary resources and attention they need to succeed. Executive buy-in can also drive your organization's alignment with and commitment to AI goals.

> **Vision communication**. Clearly communicate the vision for AI and its strategic importance to the organization. Ensure that leaders understand the challenges and potential benefits of AI adoption.

Change Management: Managing the Organizational Change Process Effectively

Effective change management is crucial for integrating AI into the organization and requires the following:

A change management plan. Develop a change management plan that addresses potential challenges and resistance to AI adoption, and include strategies for communication, training, and support.

Stakeholder engagement. Engage with stakeholders throughout the change process in a structured manner in order to address concerns and build support for AI initiatives.

Encouraging Experimentation: Promoting a Culture That Embraces Experimentation and Learning from Failures

Encouraging a culture of experimentation can drive innovation. People have to be allowed to experiment at your expense; otherwise, they're not truly fulfilling their mandates.

It's crucial that the leadership style fosters a willingness to experiment, as opposed to perpetuating a pervasive fear among a workforce too scared to take even minor risks.

The right atmosphere for a successful implementation of AI involves the following:

Innovation encouragement. You need to foster an environment where employees feel empowered to experiment with AI technologies and explore new ideas. Encourage a mindset that views failures as opportunities for learning and improvement and not as shameful episodes.

> **Support structures**. Nothings encourages people more than the actual provision of support structures like innovation labs or sandboxes where employees can test AI solutions and explore new approaches as a positive pursuit, without fear of reprisals.

Ensuring Ethical and Responsible AI Use

On the issue of ethical AI use, smart organizations globally prefer to be at the forefront of contemplating and implementing AI ethics, rather than simply following on behind those who are developing the field.

There is of course already a fairly extensive body of thought (and literature) on the topic, but AI ethics is an arena where you'll definitely want to be on the right side of history. No one knows the potential blowback from the marketplace for irresponsible use, other than the fact that it's likely to substantial.

Ethical Guidelines: Establishing Policies for Responsible AI Use

Ethical considerations are critical for ensuring responsible AI use, and organizations that want to optimize the benefits of implementation will develop the following:

> **AI ethics policies**. Develop and implement policies that outline ethical guidelines for AI use (addressing issues such as transparency, accountability, and fairness).

> **An ethical review**. Establish a review process to evaluate the ethical implications of AI projects, ensuring that AI initiatives align with your organizational values and societal norms.

Bias and Fairness: Implementing Strategies to Minimize Bias in AI Models

Minimizing bias is essential for ensuring fairness in AI, and the following considerations are paramount in making this a reality:

> **Bias detection**. You'll want to design and implement techniques for detecting and mitigating bias in AI models. Regularly assess models for potential biases and take corrective actions as needed.

> **Diverse data**. Using diverse and representative data to train AI models is your best hedge against skewed results (ensure that data sources reflect a broad range of perspectives and experiences).

Regulatory Compliance: Ensuring Compliance with Relevant Laws and Regulations

Concomitant with internal policy development is compliance with regulations that determine responsible AI use.

As with other legacy echelons of business, two points need to be brought down to manifest reality within your organization, as follows:

> **Regulatory awareness**. Stay informed about relevant laws and regulations related to AI, ensuring that your AI initiatives comply with data protection, privacy, and other standing regulatory requirements.

Compliance mechanisms. Implement mechanisms for monitoring and ensuring compliance with regulations (appoint a compliance officer to take overarching responsibility if that structure best suits your organizational hierarchy). Regularly review and update practices to align with evolving legal standards, keeping records of what changed, and why.

Conclusion

Successfully implementing Generative AI requires a strategic approach that encompasses organizational readiness, clear goal setting, investment in technology, workforce development, cultural innovation, and an ethical readiness.

By carefully assessing current capabilities, developing a focused AI strategy, investing in the right infrastructure, building a skilled workforce, fostering a culture of innovation, and ensuring ethical and responsible AI use, your organization can effectively harness the power of Generative AI.

Such a comprehensive approach not only drives competitive advantage and internal efficiency, but also fosters ongoing innovation, ensuring that your AI initiatives will align with your business goals and create lasting value.

By following these guidelines, researching real-world case studies, and keeping your organization's objectives squarely in mind, you can navigate the complexities of AI implementation and position your organization for success in an ever more AI-driven world.

CHAPTER 8

Navigating Risks and Legalities of Generative AI

As Generative AI technologies advance, understanding their associated risks and legal implications becomes increasingly crucial for business executives. There is no hiding behind automation to shield businesses from liability; indeed, there never has been, from the earliest days of the Industrial Revolution.

Generative AI's potential for crossing dangerous boundaries is no exception, but rather poses the same type of challenges to executives, although they are concerned with data privacy and the human experience of AI, instead of spoiled goods or workplace injury.

That Generative AI is going to continue infiltrating global business is beyond doubt, as it comes carrying algorithms capable of creating new content, automating complex processes, and enhancing decision-making, offering significant opportunities for innovation and efficiency.

However, the integration of these technologies into business at large introduces various risks and legal challenges that organizations must successfully address in order to ensure responsible and compliant deployment.

After a decade or two of social media scandals and panicked legislative responses around personal data, privacy, and ethical business conduct, smart organizations ensure they're proactive and vocal on the issues.

A slipshod application of Generative AI can be laden with legal ramifications, and the purpose of this chapter is to equip executives with a thorough understanding of these risks and legalities, providing a framework for navigating the complexities of Generative AI.

By exploring the key risks, legal frameworks, and mitigation strategies, executives can glean actionable insights for managing the potential pitfalls of Generative AI, while capitalizing on its benefits.

Identifying Risks in Generative AI

Generative AI presents significant opportunities for businesses, but it also brings a range of risks that must be carefully managed. The primary concerns fall into the following key areas:

> **Data privacy and security**. Businesses must address the risks associated with handling large volumes of sensitive data, including data breaches, unauthorized access, and misuse. Compliance with data protection regulations like GDPR, CCPA, and PIPEDA is crucial to mitigate these risks.

> **Intellectual property (IP) issues**. Determining the ownership and rights to AI-generated content poses challenges, particularly concerning copyright, derivative works, and patent considerations.

> **Ethical concerns**. Ensuring fairness, transparency, and accountability in AI-generated content is vital to prevent bias and discrimination, which can damage reputation and legal standing.

Operational risks. Reliability, accuracy, and potential over-reliance on AI systems are critical concerns, necessitating rigorous testing, validation, and contingency planning to ensure AI tools add value to business processes without introducing new vulnerabilities.

Understanding these risks is essential for businesses looking to leverage Generative AI effectively while maintaining compliance, safeguarding data, and upholding ethical standards.

Data Privacy and Security

Two principal issues confront modern businesses seeking to implement AI, and those are concerns around the handling of user data and its protection, and needed compliance with standing data protection legislation.

Concerns over Data Handling and Protection

Intrinsically and by design, Generative AI relies heavily on data to create and refine its outputs, making data privacy and security of paramount concern. The handling of large volumes of personal and sensitive data introduces risks related to data breaches, unauthorized access, and misuse. Key concerns on this issue include the following:

- **Data breaches**. AI systems need to process comparatively vast amounts of data, increasing the risk of breaches if security measures are inadequate. Breaches can lead to the exposure of personal information, resulting in reputational damage and open-ended financial loss.

- **Unauthorized access**. Ensuring that only authorized personnel have access to sensitive data is crucial, as inadequate access controls can lead to misuse or accidental exposure of data, whether malicious or not.

- **Misuse of data**. Then there is the possibility of the AI itself developing routes to outcomes where data is misused. Generative AI systems might inadvertently use data in ways not intended or consented to, raising concerns about data misuse.

Compliance with Data Protection Regulations

Organizations must comply with various data protection regulations to mitigate these risks. Key regulations to note include the following:

- **General Data Protection Regulation (GDPR)**. In the European Union (EU), the GDPR sets stringent requirements for data processing, including obtaining explicit consent, ensuring data accuracy, and implementing robust security measures.

- **California Consumer Privacy Act (CCPA)**. In the United States, the CCPA grants California residents rights related to their personal data, such as the right to access, delete, and opt out of the sale of their data. Compliance with CCPA requires clear data practices and user consent mechanisms. Importantly, the legislation doesn't require companies to be physically resident in California, but rather applies to all commercial entities providing goods or services to Californians, thus potentially impacting the majority of American businesses, and certainly national concerns that sell online.

- **Canadian Personal Information Protection and Electronic Documents Act (PIPEDA)**. This is a federal law governing data collection, its processing, and its protection by federal bodies and private organizations (commercial or otherwise) within Canada. These regulations were enacted as a means of assuring the global community that the Canadian private sector has complied with international standards of data management.

Intellectual Property (IP) Issues

When it comes to intellectual property rights, two principal issues emerge as challenges for organizations seeking to implement AI solutions.

Ownership of AI-Generated Content

Determining the ownership of content created by Generative AI can be complex, and this complexity is further fragmented into principal and subsequent (derived) works, as follows:

- **AI-generated content**. Content produced by AI systems may not have clear ownership under existing IP laws, and legitimate questions arise about whether the AI, its users, or the developers retain rights to content produced by the system.

- **Derivative works**. AI can generate content based on existing works, leading to potential IP rights disputes (whether the output constitutes a derivative work, and who then holds the rights).

Copyright and Patent Considerations

Generative AI also intersects with copyright and patent law, and a burgeoning new legal sector is rising to address issues such as the following:

- **Copyright**. AI-generated works may not fit neatly into traditional copyright frameworks. Opinions differ on whether AI can be an author or whether the rights automatically transfer to the human operator or developer.

- **Patents**. Innovations related to Generative AI may indeed be patentable, but the process of patenting AI inventions involves specific challenges, including demonstrating novelty and non-obviousness, among other considerations.

Ethical Concerns

Eliminating bias and ensuring fairness in Generative AI's content are crucial touch points for management, and transparency in processes with ensuing accountability are issues that will separate legitimate businesses from the rest—not necessarily a new concept, but a potentially pervasive issue for those employing AI.

Bias and Fairness in AI-Generated Content

Generative AI systems have the potential to inadvertently perpetuate or even exponentially amplify biases present in their training data, and in such systems there will be no human contemplation that might eliminate it as there would be in legacy business meetings and engagement.

Generative AI is as biased or unbiased as the data it gets, and a tweaking of inputs will need to be carefully managed in the event of discerned bias so that outputs are unbiased and valid, as follows:

- **Bias**. AI models trained on biased datasets can produce biased or discriminatory outputs, impacting fairness and inclusivity.

- **Mitigation**. Addressing bias involves using diverse and representative data, implementing bias detection mechanisms, and continuously refining models to improve fairness.

Transparency and Accountability

Ensuring transparency and accountability in AI systems is crucial, for the following reasons:

- **Transparency**. Your organization has to be willing to disclose how AI models are trained, the sources of data used, and the decision-making processes involved. Transparency helps build trust and allows for scrutiny. Smart companies will have ready answers on these issues.

- **Accountability**. Establishing unambiguous accountability for your AI-generated outcomes is crucial, and your organization must be prepared to address and rectify any negative consequences resulting from AI outputs, as indeed you would face the same obligation with legacy attributes or tools that produced similarly negative results.

Operational Risks

Commensurate with the work rate and scope of Generative AI comes an obvious need for accurate results.

You need to be able to rely on AI's outputs if they are to contribute meaningfully to business processes and profits. The benefits of Generative AI are for those who choose systems wisely (based on your detailed requirements) and feed the system correctly (more quality data is always better than less).

Reliability and Accuracy of AI-Generated Outputs

The accuracy and reliability of Generative AI outputs can impact operational effectiveness, and here is a classic case of great preparation resulting in true effectiveness:

- **Accuracy**. AI-generated outputs must be accurate and reliable to support business operations effectively, as inaccurate outputs will inevitably lead to poor decision-making and operational inefficiencies.

- **Testing and validation**. Mandatory and regularly scheduled testing and validating of AI models are necessary in order to ensure that they perform as you expected, producing results that are above all reliable.

Dependency on AI Systems

An excessive reliance on your AI systems has the potential to expose you to risks, including the following:

- **System failure**. Dependence on AI systems for critical tasks can be problematic if the systems fail or produce incorrect results. Although system failures are a variable, correct setup and inputs largely eliminate poor results. Backup plans and manual overrides should be in place nonetheless.

- **Skill gaps**. Relying heavily on AI can lead to skill gaps among employees, as their expertise may very well atrophy if AI systems handle an abundance of tasks that were traditionally performed by humans.

Legal Frameworks and Regulations

Although still in its infancy, Generative AI has already attracted regulation, in terms of both existing laws previously enacted to govern business conduct—specifically consumer data management—as well as newer legislation that has emerged to address AI's impact on commerce and industry.

Current Legal Landscape

Although not tumultuous, Generative AI's impact on standing legislation is already being felt, and will grow in import and volume as we move into a greater assimilation of AI by global business.

Overview of Existing Laws and Regulations Affecting Generative AI

The legal landscape for Generative AI is evolving, with several existing laws impacting its use, including the following:

- **Data protection laws**. Regulations like GDPR and CCPA govern how organizations handle and protect personal data, in turn influencing how Generative AI systems manage and process data.

- **IP laws**. Intellectual property laws, including copyright and patent regulations, affect the ownership and protection of AI-generated content and innovations, although several precedents have yet to be established in this arena.

- **Consumer protection laws**. Laws related to consumer protection ensure that AI systems do not mislead or harm consumers, particularly in areas like advertising and product recommendations.

Key International Regulations and Standards

In keeping with the most prominent regulations listed earlier in Point 1.1.2, there are also current standards and emerging mores and norms that pertain to Generative AI employment, as follows:

- **OECD Principles on AI**. The Organization for Economic Co-operation and Development (OECD) has formulated principles concerning AI usage, emphasizing transparency, responsible stewardship, and accountability.

- **ISO Standards**. The International Standards Organization (ISO) has also developed standards for AI that address quality, safety, and risk management.

Future Legal Developments

The employment of Generative AI by ever more commercial and other entities is undoubtedly going to lead to a quickening stream of impact on extant legal regulation pertaining to AI.

Anticipated Changes in Legislation

Future developments in legislation may impact Generative AI in the following ways:

- **AI-specific regulations**. Governments and regulatory bodies are considering new regulations tailored specifically for AI technologies. These regulations will deal with issues like AI ethics, transparency, and accountability.

- **Cross-border data transfer**. Regulations on cross-border data transfer will evolve, impacting how organizations manage and transfer data used by AI systems across different jurisdictions, effectively building a chain of custody specific to the employment of AI systems.

Emerging Legal Trends and Their Potential Impact

Emerging legal trends will certainly influence the Generative AI landscape, and key areas will include the following:

- **AI liability**. Legal frameworks are beginning to address liability issues related to AI, including who the responsible parties are when harm is caused by AI systems.

- **AI transparency requirements**. Increasing demands for transparency in AI decision-making processes are likely to lead to new requirements for disclosing AI algorithms and training data.

Mitigating Risks

The implementation of Generative AI comes with far greater benefits than risks, and it's possible to mitigate those risks through established and intuitive practices.

Implementing Robust Data Governance

Few companies on the cusp of AI deployment will be naive on the issue of data management and governance. Because the volume and quality of data required to successfully employ Generative AI is a new level of operation for many, however, watertight data control is paramount.

Best Practices for Data Management

Practical and effective data governance is essential for managing data privacy and security, and this begins with the following:

- **Data classification**. Classify data based on sensitivity, and apply appropriate benchmark security measures. This helps ensure that sensitive data receives the highest level of protection. Make no mistake—bad actors are evolving alongside AI as sure as the sun rises and sets.

- **Access controls**. Implement strict access controls to limit data access to authorized personnel only, and you should regularly review and update access permissions.

- **Data encryption**. You need to employ encryption to protect data when at rest and when in transit. Encryption helps prevent unauthorized access and can devalue or nullify data breaches.

Ensuring Data Quality and Integrity

Maintaining data quality and integrity is crucial for effective AI operations, and points to consider include the following:

- **Data accuracy**. Data should be regularly validated and cleaned to ensure accuracy. Inaccurate data can lead to flawed AI outputs and decision-making—regular inspection avoids greater woes down the line.

- **Data integrity**. Implement measures to protect data from unauthorized alterations or other potential corruption. Ensure also that data remains consistent and reliable throughout its lifecycle.

Ensuring Compliance

Legislation will no doubt evolve into broader laws with more clarity, making it easier to comply with relevant legislation, but for now it's best to overcompensate in terms of compliance (rather than find yourself outside of what is considered legal).

This is a cost consideration and need not be taken to a ridiculous extreme, but it *is* essential that you demonstrate your knowledge of and compliance with standing legislation that impacts your operations.

Strategies for Staying Compliant with Regulations

Regulatory compliance is crucial to avoid potential legal pitfalls, and can be achieved by the following:

- **Regular audits**. Conduct regular audits to assess compliance with data protection and IP regulations so that you can identify and address any compliance gaps.

- **Legal consultations**. Engage legal experts to interpret and apply regulations *accurately*. Legal consultations can provide guidance on navigating complex regulatory environments, and an accurate application of the law is more cost-effective than a shotgun approach.

Role of Legal and Compliance Teams

Legal and compliance teams play a critical role in ensuring adherence to regulations, and recommended tolls and processes include the following:

- **Compliance frameworks**. You need to develop and implement compliance frameworks that outline procedures and responsibilities for adhering to relevant laws.

- **Training and awareness**. You should also provide training to employees on compliance requirements and best practices. Raising awareness helps ensure that all stakeholders understand their roles in maintaining compliance.

Addressing Ethical Concerns

There are persistent ethical concerns surrounding the use of AI, and while some may be overblown, this does not delegitimize the issue.

The benefits of Generative AI are best experienced devoid of legal wrangles or ethical tainting, and with some basic tools in place, it's entirely possible to be on the right side of the issue.

Developing Ethical Guidelines for AI Use

Establishing ethical guidelines helps ensure responsible AI use. Effective AI ethics management can include the following:

- **Ethical framework**. Develop an ethical framework that outlines principles for AI use, including fairness, transparency, and accountability. You need to ensure that your AI practices align with your organizational values and societal expectations.

- **Ethical review boards**. Consider setting up ethical review boards to evaluate and oversee AI projects. These boards can provide guidance on ethical dilemmas while ensuring that projects adhere to ethical standards.

Promoting Transparency and Accountability

Transparency and accountability are essential for maintaining trust, and just as with legacy components of organizational operation, the following attributes are indispensable:

- **Transparent practices**. You should be able to clearly communicate how AI models are developed, trained, and used, and willing to provide information on data sources, algorithms, and decision-making processes.

- **Accountability mechanisms**. Establish mechanisms for addressing and rectifying issues related to AI outputs, and ensure that there are *clear lines of accountability* for AI-generated outcomes.

Enhancing Operational Resilience

Again in acknowledgment of the volume of data that will be in play, as well as the reliance you will place on Generative AI's outcomes, enhancing operational resilience becomes more than a nice-to-have-it's essential.

Building Robust AI Systems

Developing resilient AI systems is critical for minimizing operational risks, and this begins with the following:

- **System testing**. Conduct thorough testing of AI systems to identify and address potential issues before deployment. Regularly test and update systems to ensure continued reliable performance.

- **Fail-safes**. Implement fail-safes and backup mechanisms to manage potential system failures. Ensure that there are contingency plans in place for maintaining operations during potential AI system outages.

Regular Monitoring and Evaluation

Ongoing monitoring and evaluation are key to maintaining operational resilience, and comprise the following:

- **Performance monitoring**. Continuously monitor AI systems to assess their performance and accuracy (implement monitoring tools to detect and address issues promptly).

- **Periodic reviews**. Conduct periodic reviews of your AI systems to evaluate their effectiveness and make necessary adjustments. Regular reviews help ensure that systems remain aligned with both your business goals *and* regulatory requirements.

Best Practices for Business Executives

The following points together constitute the ideal toolbox with which your Generative AI implementation will be both successful and safe. With these in play, it becomes easier to focus on tweaking the benefits, which, after all, is the ultimate value of deployment.

Risk Assessment and Management

For many business sectors, this is custom and best practice. Knowing your risks and managing them successfully entails several aspects.

Conducting Thorough Risk Assessments

Risk assessments are essential for identifying and managing potential risks, and should center on the following main aspects:

- **Risk identification**. Identify potential risks related to data privacy, IP, ethics, and operations, using risk assessment tools and methodologies to evaluate the likelihood and impact of each risk.

- **Risk mitigation**. You also need to develop and implement risk mitigation strategies to address identified risks, prioritizing risks based on their potential impact and likelihood, and allocate resources accordingly.

Developing Risk Management Strategies

Effective risk management strategies help mitigate potential issues, and should include the following:

- **Risk management plan**. Create a comprehensive risk management plan that outlines strategies for managing and mitigating risks, including procedures for responding to and recovering from risk events.

- **Contingency planning**. Develop contingency plans for handling unexpected issues related to AI systems, and ensure that plans are regularly reviewed and updated.

Legal and Ethical Considerations

Legal issues surrounding Generative AI are both complex and often novel, and smart AI deployment should see the retention or at least engagement of specific legal expertise at the outset.

Generative AI implementation is most cost-effectively done with foreknowledge of all relevant legal implications—having to straighten things up post-implementation is not only a waste of time and money, but also simply delays any return on the investment.

Engaging Legal Experts

Legal experts play a crucial role in navigating the legal complexities of Generative AI, and engaging relevant expertise should take the form of the following:

- **Legal consultation**. Consult with legal experts to understand and address legal requirements related to AI use. The right legal experts can provide guidance on compliance, IP issues, and regulatory changes.

- **Legal reviews**. Conduct legal reviews of AI projects and practices to ensure that they adhere to relevant laws and regulations, in consultation with your legal help. Regular reviews help identify and address potential legal issues, develop your book of knowledge of safe practices, and quash issues before they arise.

Establishing an Ethical AI Framework

An ethical AI framework guides responsible AI use, and the following components will build this framework:

- **Ethical principles**. Develop a set of ethical principles that govern the use of AI within your organization, ensuring that these principles address key ethical concerns like fairness, transparency, and accountability.

- **Ethics committees**. Consider establishing ethics committees to oversee AI projects and ensure that they align with ethical guidelines. These committees can provide valuable insights and recommendations, and act as a soft foil that eliminates much of the potential for gross errors.

Continuous Monitoring and Improvement

Frequently a concept merely paid lip service in other echelons of legacy business, continuous monitoring and improvement is mandatory, and essentially in-built, with Generative AI.

Importance of Ongoing Monitoring

Ongoing monitoring is crucial for managing risks and ensuring compliance, and happens within the following principal structures:

- **Real-time monitoring**. Implement real-time monitoring systems to track AI performance and detect potential issues. Continuous monitoring helps identify and address problems before they escalate.

- **Feedback loops**. Create feedback loops to gather input from stakeholders and users, and use feedback to make informed adjustments and improvements to your AI systems.

Adapting to Changes in the Legal and Regulatory Landscape

The legal and regulatory landscape of AI is continuously evolving, and often heads over novel and legally complex terrain.

In conjunction with the practices outlined earlier, staying informed of relevant legal developments and court precedents can keep you at the forefront of best practice, as follows:

- **Regulatory updates**. Stay informed about changes in regulations and standards that affect AI, regularly reviewing and updating compliance practices to align with new requirements.

- **Legal adaptation**. Be prepared to adapt legal and operational practices in response to evolving legal trends and emerging regulations. Flexibility and adaptability are key to maintaining compliance and managing AI's risks effectively.

Conclusion

Navigating the risks and legalities of Generative AI requires a comprehensive approach that encompasses understanding data privacy, intellectual property, ethical concerns, and operational risks.

By staying informed about current and evolving legal frameworks, while implementing robust risk mitigation strategies, *and* adhering to best practices, you can effectively manage the complexities associated with Generative AI.

The integration of Generative AI offers significant opportunities for innovation and efficiency, but it also demands careful consideration of legal and ethical implications.

By proactively addressing these challenges, organizations can leverage Generative AI technology responsibly and effectively, ensuring alignment with legal requirements and ethical standards, while gleaning all of the benefits and driving business success.

Evaluating the Success of Generative AI Initiatives

As Generative AI continues to revolutionize product development and business processes, a critical question emerges for executives: How do we measure the success of our Generative AI initiatives? In an era where AI capabilities are advancing rapidly, it's crucial to have robust frameworks and metrics in place to evaluate the impact and effectiveness of these powerful tools.

This chapter aims to provide business executives with a comprehensive guide to measuring Generative AI deployments. We'll explore various frameworks, suggest potential metrics, and offer insights into best practices for evaluation. By the end of this chapter, you'll be equipped with the knowledge and tools to assess your Generative AI initiatives effectively, ensuring that your investments in this transformative technology yield tangible business value.

The Challenge of Evaluating Generative AI

Evaluating the success of Generative AI initiatives presents unique challenges compared to traditional technology implementations. The open-ended nature of generative models, their ability to produce

© Ahmed Bouzid, Paolo Narciso, Weiye Ma 2024
A. Bouzid et al., *Generative AI For Executives*,
https://doi.org/10.1007/979-8-8688-0950-7_9

diverse outputs, and the often subjective quality of these outputs make standardized evaluation difficult. Moreover, the impact of Generative AI can extend beyond immediate productivity gains to influence broader aspects of organizational culture, innovation capacity, and even societal impacts.

Recent research has highlighted the multifaceted nature of Generative AI evaluation. Weidinger and colleagues (2023) propose a sociotechnical approach that goes beyond mere capability assessments to consider human interaction and systemic impacts. This underscores the need for a holistic evaluation framework that considers not only the technical performance of AI systems but also their broader implications for your organization and society at large.

Frameworks for Evaluating Generative AI

To address the complexities of Generative AI evaluation, several frameworks have been proposed. Let's explore some of the most promising approaches.

The Sociotechnical Evaluation Framework

Weidinger and colleagues (2023) suggest a three-layered sociotechnical approach to evaluating Generative AI. The first layer focuses on capability evaluations, assessing the technical performance of the AI system. This involves evaluating the model's ability to perform specific tasks, such as text generation, code completion, or image creation. Metrics in this layer might include accuracy, relevance, and coherence of outputs.

The second layer examines human interaction, considering how users engage with the AI system. It looks at factors such as ease of use, user satisfaction, and the system's ability to understand and respond to user intent. Metrics here could include user engagement rates, time saved, and qualitative feedback on user experience.

The final layer explores systemic impacts, looking at the broader implications of the AI system on your organization and society. This includes considerations of ethical use, potential biases, and long-term effects on workforce skills and job roles. Metrics in this layer are often more qualitative and might include assessments of workforce adaptation, changes in organizational culture, and alignment with ethical AI principles.

This framework provides a comprehensive view of Generative AI impact, encouraging executives to look beyond immediate performance metrics to consider the wider implications of AI deployment.

The Social Impact Evaluation Framework

Solaiman and colleagues (2023) propose a framework for evaluating the social impacts of Generative AI across various categories. This framework is particularly useful for organizations concerned with the ethical implications and societal effects of their AI initiatives. Key categories for evaluation include fairness and non-discrimination, privacy and data protection, transparency and explainability, safety and security, environmental impact, labor and economic impact, and cultural and social impact.

For each category, the framework suggests specific metrics and evaluation methods. For instance, under fairness and non-discrimination, you might assess your AI system for bias in its outputs across different demographic groups. Under environmental impact, you could measure the energy consumption and carbon footprint of your AI models. This framework helps ensure that your Generative AI initiatives align with corporate social responsibility goals and mitigate potential negative societal impacts.

The CBDAS Data Maturity Model

Malacaria and colleagues (2023) adapt the CBDAS (Capability, Business, Data, Analytics, Scale) data maturity model for evaluating Generative AI initiatives. This model focuses on organizational readiness and maturity in deploying AI technologies. It assesses the technical skills and infrastructure needed for AI deployment, evaluates the alignment of AI initiatives with business goals and processes, examines the quality, quantity, and management of data used to train and operate AI models, assesses the organization's ability to derive insights from AI outputs, and evaluates the organization's capacity to deploy AI solutions at scale.

This model helps executives understand their organization's strengths and weaknesses in AI deployment, guiding investment decisions and improvement efforts.

The GreatAI Framework

Schmelczer and Visser (2023) developed the GreatAI framework, which focuses specifically on natural language processing (NLP) applications of Generative AI. This framework implements 33 best practices across several key areas, including data quality and management, model selection and training, output evaluation and refinement, user interface and experience, and ethical considerations and governance.

The GreatAI framework provides a practical, actionable approach to implementing and evaluating Generative AI initiatives, particularly those focused on text-generation and language-comprehension tasks.

Key Metrics for Evaluating Generative AI

While the specific metrics you use will depend on your chosen framework and the nature of your Generative AI application, there are several key metrics to consider across different dimensions.

In terms of technical performance, it's crucial to measure the output quality, assessing the relevance, coherence, and accuracy of AI-generated content. This could involve human evaluation or automated metrics like BLEU scores for text generation.

BLEU, which stands for Bilingual Evaluation Understudy, is an algorithm for evaluating the quality of text that has been machine-translated from one language to another. However, it has also been adapted for use in evaluating other types of text-generation tasks, including those performed by Generative AI.

BLEU works by comparing a candidate text (the AI-generated output) to one or more reference texts (typically human-written). The core idea is to measure how many words and phrases the candidate text shares with the reference texts. The more overlap there is, the higher the BLEU score.

Response time is another important metric, evaluating the speed at which the AI system generates outputs, particularly important for real-time applications. Scalability should also be assessed, looking at the system's ability to handle increased load and maintain performance as usage grows. Tracking error rates, or the frequency of errors or inappropriate outputs, can indicate areas for model improvement.

Business impact metrics are essential for justifying AI investments. These include productivity gains, measuring time saved or output increased due to AI assistance. For example, you might track the reduction in time spent on content creation or code writing. Cost savings calculations should consider the financial impact of AI deployment, including reduced labor costs or improved resource allocation. Revenue impact assessments look at any increase in sales or new revenue streams directly attributable to AI-enhanced products or services. The innovation rate can be tracked by measuring the number of new ideas or products developed with AI assistance compared to traditional methods.

User experience metrics provide insights into how well the AI system is serving its intended users. User satisfaction can be gauged through surveys or analysis of user feedback regarding AI-generated outputs and interactions. The adoption rate measures the percentage of eligible users actively using the AI system and tracks usage trends over time. Assessing the learning curve helps one understand how quickly users become proficient with the AI system, which can indicate ease of use and effective integration. Evaluating customization and personalization capabilities shows the AI system's ability to adapt to individual user preferences and needs.

Ethical and social impact metrics are increasingly important as AI systems become more prevalent. Regular bias assessments test for and measure any biases in AI outputs across different demographic groups or topics. Privacy compliance tracking ensures adherence to data protection regulations and monitors any breaches or near-misses. A transparency score can be developed to measure how well the AI system can explain its decisions or provide sources for its outputs. Environmental impact assessments should measure the energy consumption and carbon footprint of your AI models and infrastructure.

Long-term strategic metrics help align AI initiatives with broader organizational goals. Competitive advantage assessments compare your AI capabilities to industry benchmarks and competitors. Skill development tracking measures the growth of AI-related skills within your workforce. Organizational agility metrics evaluate how AI deployment affects your organization's ability to respond to market changes and new opportunities. Brand perception monitoring can reveal changes related to your AI initiatives, particularly in terms of innovation and ethical leadership.

Implementing an Evaluation Framework

To effectively evaluate your Generative AI initiatives, a structured approach is necessary. Begin by selecting an appropriate framework that aligns with your organizational goals and the specific nature of your AI deployment. You may need to combine elements from multiple frameworks for a comprehensive evaluation. Clearly define your objectives, articulating what success looks like for your Generative AI initiative. This could range from specific productivity improvements to broader innovation goals.

Establish baseline measurements before deploying your AI system, measuring current performance across relevant metrics to provide a basis for comparison. Implement continuous monitoring by setting up systems to constantly collect data on your chosen metrics. This may involve a combination of automated data collection and regular human assessments.

Conduct regular reviews by scheduling periodic assessments of your AI initiative's performance against your defined objectives and metrics. Be prepared to adjust your approach based on these insights. Engage a diverse group of stakeholders in the evaluation process, including end users, technical teams, business leaders, and ethics experts. Use the insights gained from your evaluations to continuously refine your AI models, deployment strategies, and even your evaluation framework itself.

Case Study: Evaluating a Generative AI Content Creation Tool

To illustrate how these evaluation principles might be applied in practice, let's consider a hypothetical case study of a media company implementing a Generative AI tool for content creation. The company's objective is to increase content production efficiency while maintaining quality and adhering to ethical standards. They decide to use a combination of the Sociotechnical Evaluation Framework and elements from the GreatAI framework.

Key metrics for this initiative span several categories. Technical performance metrics include output quality (measured by expert review and engagement metrics), content generation speed, and plagiarism detection rate. Business impact is assessed through time saved in the content creation process, increase in content volume, and cost savings in content production. User experience metrics encompass writer satisfaction with AI assistance (survey-based), AI tool adoption rate among writing staff, and the learning curve for new users. Ethical and social impact is evaluated through bias assessment in generated content, transparency of AI contribution in published articles, and adherence to journalistic ethics (expert review). Long-term strategic impact is measured by reader perception of content quality and brand innovation, development of AI skills among writing staff, and competitive positioning in the digital media landscape.

The evaluation process begins with baseline measurement, capturing current content production rates, costs, and quality metrics before deployment. A phased rollout introduces the AI tool to a small team first, allowing for close monitoring and adjustment. Continuous monitoring systems track quantitative metrics like content volume and generation speed, while regular surveys capture user experience data. Monthly reviews assess performance against objectives, with quarterly deep dives including ethical audits and strategic alignment checks. Regular feedback sessions with writers, editors, and readers gather qualitative insights. Based on evaluation results, the company fine-tunes the AI model, adjusts usage guidelines, and provides targeted training to maximize benefits while mitigating risks.

After six months, the evaluation reveals a 30% increase in content production volume, a 25% reduction in time spent on initial drafts, and a 90% writer adoption rate with high satisfaction scores. Quality scores are maintained with a slight increase in originality ratings, and no significant increase in detected bias is observed, with improved consistency in style guide adherence. Reader feedback on content freshness is positive, though some concerns about transparency of AI use are noted.

These results allow the company to demonstrate clear ROI from the AI initiative while also identifying areas for further improvement, such as enhancing transparency around AI use in content creation.

Challenges and Considerations

While frameworks and metrics provide a solid foundation for evaluating Generative AI initiatives, several challenges and considerations remain. The subjectivity in evaluation is a key issue, as many aspects of Generative AI output, particularly in creative domains, are inherently subjective. Balancing quantitative metrics with qualitative assessments is crucial.

The rapidly evolving capabilities of Generative AI technologies mean that evaluation frameworks and metrics may need frequent updating to remain relevant. Unintended consequences pose another challenge, as some impacts of Generative AI may only become apparent over time. This necessitates long-term monitoring and flexibility in evaluation approaches.

Ensuring ethical use of AI goes beyond mere compliance checks. It requires ongoing dialogue and sometimes difficult trade-offs between different ethical principles. Data privacy is another critical consideration, as evaluation processes often require access to user data or AI outputs, which must be handled in compliance with data protection regulations and ethical standards.

The lack of comparative benchmarks presents a challenge, as Generative AI is still an emerging field, making it difficult to assess relative success. Resource allocation is an ongoing issue, as comprehensive evaluation of Generative AI initiatives can be resource-intensive. Balancing the depth of evaluation with practical constraints requires careful consideration.

Future Directions in Generative AI Evaluation

As the field of Generative AI continues to evolve, so too will the approaches to evaluating its impact. Emerging trends and future directions include the development of more-sophisticated automated evaluation tools that can assess the quality and impact of AI-generated outputs across various domains. Industry-wide initiatives to standardize evaluation metrics and frameworks are likely to emerge, allowing for better benchmarking and comparison across organizations.

Interdisciplinary approaches are gaining traction, with increasing collaboration between technologists, ethicists, social scientists, and domain experts to develop more holistic evaluation methodologies. There's a move toward real-time evaluation of AI systems, allowing for immediate adjustments and interventions. User-centric evaluation is receiving greater emphasis, with more focus on capturing and analyzing user experiences and perceptions in evaluating AI systems.

The development of more-robust methodologies for assessing the broader societal impacts of widespread Generative AI adoption is an area of growing importance. As AI systems become more adaptive and context-aware, evaluation frameworks will need to evolve to assess these dynamic capabilities.

Conclusion

Evaluating the success of Generative AI initiatives is a complex but crucial task for business executives. By adopting comprehensive evaluation frameworks and carefully selected metrics, organizations can ensure that their investments in AI technology deliver tangible business value while aligning with ethical standards and long-term strategic goals.

The frameworks and metrics discussed in this chapter provide a starting point for developing a robust evaluation strategy. However, the rapidly evolving nature of Generative AI means that evaluation approaches must remain flexible and adaptable. Regular reassessment of your evaluation framework, staying informed about new developments in AI assessment, and maintaining open dialogue with stakeholders are key to long-term success.

Remember that the goal of evaluation is not just to measure performance, but to drive continuous improvement and responsible innovation. By thoughtfully evaluating your Generative AI initiatives, you can unlock the full potential of this transformative technology, creating value for your organization while navigating the ethical and societal implications of AI deployment.

As you embark on or continue your Generative AI journey, let robust evaluation be your guide, ensuring that your initiatives not only meet immediate business objectives but also contribute positively to your organization's long-term success and societal impact.

CHAPTER 10

Looking Ahead: Preparing for the Future of Generative AI

The rise of Generative AI is clearly set to become one of the most significant forces shaping the future of business. As this technology continues to advance, it is fundamentally altering industries and transforming traditional business operations. This chapter explores the critical role of strategic technology investments in harnessing the power of Generative AI, focusing on the breakthroughs in quantum and neuromorphic computing that are pushing the boundaries of what AI can achieve. Additionally, the chapter examines the emergence of new AI paradigms, such as federated learning and explainable AI, which are becoming essential tools for businesses to enhance efficiency, security, and transparency. By understanding and integrating these cutting-edge technologies and approaches, organizations can position themselves to not only adapt to the rapidly changing landscape but also to innovate and maintain a competitive advantage in the market.

© Ahmed Bouzid, Paolo Narciso, Weiye Ma 2024
A. Bouzid et al., *Generative AI For Executives*,
https://doi.org/10.1007/979-8-8688-0950-7_10

Capitalizing on Emerging AI Trends

In today's fast-evolving technological landscape, AI stands out as a key disruptor, fundamentally transforming how businesses operate and compete. From enhancing decision-making to streamlining operations, AI presents a strategic opportunity for organizations that recognize its potential early. To stay ahead, businesses must invest in emerging AI trends like quantum computing, neuromorphic computing, federated learning, and explainable AI (XAI). These innovations provide competitive advantages by boosting performance, enhancing security, and building trust, helping companies navigate market disruptions and maintain a leading edge in their industries.

Strategic Technology Investment

Market disruptions don't happen every day. However, when they do, everything turns upside-down. These changes, whether a service or product or belief, fundamentally reshape systems and processes, including even the daily mundane. Artificial intelligence, or AI, is one of those market disrupters. It starts small and then grows, spreading exponentially. The businesses that pay attention to these elements stay ahead of the curve strategically, finding ways to harness the advantages of AI before others.

Quantum Computing: Opportunities for Competitive Advantage

At the end of the spectrum where high-powered computers are found, quantum computing is the name of the game now. Unlike standard computers, which have been using an architecture of bits that's been around since at least the 1970s, quantum computing makes a leap forward with qubits. What's so special about that difference? Qubits "multitask" processing and memory-producing at the same time. This duality allows for a much higher level of performance, faster and broader, just the kind of powerhouse that allows AI to come into its own faster.

The possibilities for companies that need to use technology to stay ahead are obvious; quantum computing allows for a larger data pool to be processed, and that leads to more-powerful machine learning and problem solving. A scale of operation similar to what Amazon is experiencing through traditional database automation becomes possible for everyone else. And it can be applied to different disciplines that rely heavily on processing. For example, pharmaceutical development depends on protein processing, which can take weeks with traditional computers. It becomes days and hours with quantum computing and AI. Financing, marketing, and more can all benefit from the same.

Neuromorphic Computing: Enhancing AI Capabilities

The next evolution of AI comes in the form of reaching for a thinking model, where AI does the creative problem-solving versus just processing data. Dubbed "neuromorphic" computing, this approach works off of the neural network design that emulates how the human brain operates. The benefits of the neuromorphic design allow AI to be adaptive versus just responsive, and that starts to go down the path of actual learning. While AI behavior is not sentient by any means, the advancements being made with neuromorphic computing are paving the way for AI identity recognition, speech comprehension, and autonomous system management. These too become the foundation for what's to come in the next decade.

Companies that look for ways to integrate neuromorphic designs will be the early winners in the next stage of AI performance. And that can put a company in the pivotal position of being the provider for other users, much the same way tool merchants created business gateways serving gold miners in the 1840s and the Gold Rush.

Innovative AI Paradigms

Business processes are typically based on paradigms, or models of approach. These are powerful frameworks that dictate business behavior as an organization and even as a market. AI, however, introduces new paradigms that can augment human processes or create new ones that don't require human involvement.

Federated Learning: Securing Data While Enhancing Performance

The internet has fully embraced the advantages of decentralized computing, especially with blockchain technology. While decentralized computing is still making roots for greater utility, it's at the edge of the envelope in terms of new development. AI's being able to operate in these kinds of environments is now known as "federated learning." The combination boosts far more solid data integrity, blocks fraud because of multiple points of verification that can't be hacked from one centralized point, and keeps sensitive information protected without proper authorization to access.

By building federated learning systems for a company's AI tool, teams can leverage AI where it excels with multi-tasking across networks. Healthcare now uses the approach for predictive management and anticipating peak demand points for better efficiency. Patient privacy is protected all along the way, but the service delivery improves by multiple factors.

Explainable AI (XAI): Improving Trust and Transparency in AI Decisions

The worry of using AI tends to be due to a misunderstanding about how it actually operates. Company managers can feel hesitant to engage because the mechanics of the tool aren't clear in terms of how it arrives at its output. Explainable AI, or XAI, bridges the gap between AI's being a "black box" and its being a transparent, powerful tool. The clarity provided by XAI technology helps cut through the fog with regulators as well as major account users, both of which have an impact on a company's success. This difference in confidence matters in industries like investment finance, capital funding, mergers and acquisitions, and similar. In the medical field, XAI helps bolster support for AI-supported diagnoses, increasing use with consistent performance in patient outcomes.

People work better with the familiar; the unknown tends to create anxiety. So, the more people understand AI, the faster it shifts from an unknown to a usable advantage.

Future-Proofing the Workforce

The future of talent management goes beyond traditional skill development, particularly with the increasing integration of artificial intelligence (AI) in the workplace. While AI is often perceived as merely a tool for simplifying mundane tasks like writing memos, its potential reaches much further. When employees are trained in leveraging AI's capabilities, they begin to evolve their roles, driving better results and enabling companies to redefine positions with a focus on creative and complex work.

AI's integration helps shift routine responsibilities—such as data processing, monitoring, and quality control—away from human workers, allowing them to concentrate on innovative and strategic endeavors. By embracing AI's potential, organizations can open up new job opportunities, foster continuous learning, and create dynamic, adaptable workforces that are better equipped to achieve new targets and breakthroughs. Engaging with AI-driven learning programs and integrating AI skills into training curricula are essential steps in this evolution, ensuring the workforce remains competitive and aligned with the demands of the future.

Evolving Talent Management

The inclusion of AI within the workplace has generally been associated with being a fancy search engine for quick memo-writing. That said, office-based AI goes a lot further than just being an automated letter-writer. By training employees in all the current possibilities of how they can use AI, the same people start to evolve their skills, producing better results.

Redefining Roles with AI Integration

While it's true that AI finds immediate application in shortening the work time on basic tasks like writing, drafting code, or processing data, it also frees people up to do far more with complexity. Giving you more time to focus on challenging concepts, AI takes care of the mundane in the meantime that just has to be periodically addressed and can't be ignored. Things like routine quality control, monitoring, testing, and monotonous processing all can be handled by AI, freeing up people to deal with the creative side and process improvement. Companies that focus on pushing their people into new skills and challenges for higher productivity typically realize an adaptable workforce that consistently hits new targets. Redefining roles shouldn't be avoided; it should be engaged with purpose, using AI to push people off the boring branch and get them flying again.

Creating New AI-Centric Job Opportunities

While AI will make redundant functions just described easy to replace, with automation running 24/7, it also can create new functions and possibilities for a workforce. Because AI takes what otherwise would have required programming, artistic talent, and experience or writing capability and puts it in a person's hands within seconds or minutes, the tool also allows more people to achieve new designs, builds, and products they otherwise never would have produced. More people will find they now have the ability do functions they previously were blocked out of by basic entry-level skill capacity. And since new market breakthroughs happen with the creative side, not the redundant side, the change increases the probability of new breakthroughs for the business involved.

Continuous Learning and Development

Companies that have engaged with AI need to remember that it's a process of continuous learning, especially right now with AI being new and under ongoing development. Each year right now brings a new wave of advancement and additional learning for users. As a result, investment in AI also means investing in people's continuing education with the tool.

Implementing AI-Driven Learning Programs

Agreeing people should be trained and then making it happen are two different things, however. Especially with innovative technology, finding the training expertise that can deliver correctly and accurately can be a bit of a challenge. Adaptive learning platforms can help in this regard, providing training that is tailored to how fast AI can change and evolve. Upskilling a workforce doesn't need to be a stab in the dark; using a targeted learning approach that stays current with AI improvements shows support of a company's workforce for the long term. People feel valued, and they return it with loyalty as well.

Incorporating AI Skills into Training Curricula

Training teams in companies shouldn't just stop with AI either. By providing a broad understanding of how elements of AI work, as well as how data is managed and produced, businesses can realize capital investments in key personnel. Additional areas to consider include data science, programming logic versus coding per se, database management, and similar. Related training dividends come back with new products and services these employees think up with their new skills.

Building a Scalable AI Infrastructure

To leverage AI effectively, companies need a robust and scalable infrastructure that can adapt to the growing demands of AI technologies. Most companies today operate on either traditional or hybrid networks, with a few being fully cloud-based. As AI adoption grows, businesses must upgrade their systems to support increased data storage, computing power, and networking capabilities. Cloud networks offer a scalable and cost-efficient solution, enabling companies to expand without the sunk costs associated with traditional infrastructure.

AI's growth is further bolstered by integrating smart infrastructures, such as Internet of Things (IoT) networks, which provide real-time data and allow AI systems to control and adjust operations dynamically. This seamless integration can lead to quicker improvements, better decision-making, and increased operational efficiency, benefiting companies of all sizes.

To maximize AI's potential, companies should also consider industry-wide standardization and public–private partnerships, which foster compatibility, growth, and shared innovation. Additionally, collaborating with global AI research entities can unlock new market opportunities and bring diverse expertise into the fold, enhancing a company's competitive edge.

Investing in AI-Ready Environments

AI sees its greatest performance with companies that have a robust infrastructure to house it. Additionally, that same system needs to be scalable as changes occur over time.

Developing Smart Infrastructures for AI Deployment

The typical company system right now falls into two categories: either a traditional network design or a hybrid approach with a combination of traditional network and cloud. A few are 100 percent cloud-based, but these are fairly new or startups using cloud scaling to their advantage.

Companies that jump in with both feet for AI also update their infrastructure to handle AI's growth. Scalable features provide the ability to take on more data storage, more computing, and more networking as AI demand grows and its capability gets better. Cloud networks are particularly advantageous in this arena since scalability is already a fundamental feature of such systems. And the cost to either migrate to or add a cloud system is minimal. The business is only charged what it needs, unlike sunk resources in a traditional system.

As AI evolves into a company's needs, a matching infrastructure on the IT side clears the path for its growth and additional integration into business processes. People avoid being frustrated by technology compatibility issues they can't control. Those issues get removed ahead of time. Instead, AI becomes fundamental to how people work, and when they find new uses or the AI evolves to a better version, it seamlessly advances the whole.

Enhancing IoT Networks to Support AI Systems

A definitive area that enhances AI in the physical process world involves the Internet of Things, or IoT. This involves the hardware that is already predesigned to be programmed and integrated with the internet. Because of those features, AI can then be directed to control such equipment and operate it within expected parameters 24/7, as well as to make adjustments as variables become introduced, such as temperature change, changing monitoring conditions, demand fluctuations, power spikes, and wear and tear.

By matching IoT-ready equipment to a company AI-powered network, businesses now have the ability to both affect processes as well as see objective feedback without biases. The raw data doesn't lie; inefficiencies stick out like sore thumbs, and improvements happen faster as a result. And businesses of all sizes can benefit. No one needs to be the size of Amazon or IBM to quickly take advantage.

Strengthening Industry Collaborations

Standardization within an industry also helps all involved. While being unique definitely creates growth advantages in marketing, production and operations benefit when everyone involved in the same market uses AI and IoT together. The market environment finds compatibility and growth in partnerships and commonality.

Public–Private Partnerships for AI Advancements

An under-utilized area for companies but one readily available with growth opportunity tends to be public–private partnerships. Government and nonprofits want to see economies grow that produce jobs, community improvement, and income. So, they are both quite willing to help support new private AI ventures that turnaround expansion in community benefits. Technology has been one of those areas that public policy likes to embrace with grants and joint power-authority projects. Focused on ground-breaking research, proving applicability of theoretical technology, and job creation, public–private partnerships can help with capital investment, allowing a business to venture into AI without bearing the entire cost alone. It ends up being a win–win for all involved.

Collaborating with Global AI Research Entities

International collaboration opens up both expertise as well as new market opportunities when companies find ways to work with international partners via AI advancement. The field is wide open for companies to find common bridges across borders, and these too end up finding government support to encourage additional trade activity. Because AI is so decentralized now in application, there is little in terms of proprietary concerns; so, collaboration makes sense, using the ant-hill philosophy that the many are stronger than the one.

By finding collaboration opportunities through AI and international industry associations, companies can tap into foreign talent, find new selling channels, and bring technology skills back home as well.

Unlocking New Business Opportunities

AI in Emerging Markets

AI has been particularly explosive in international markets where businesses may not have the deep resources to enjoy significant networks and IT infrastructure in-house. These markets tend to have a higher number of smaller businesses, entrepreneurs, and local networking. AI has been a godsend to many companies in these arenas, helping fill the gaps where resources aren't available or too expensive to fill in. Just like the cloud, AI gives exponential opportunity for emerging markets.

AI Solutions for Untapped Market Segments

The popularity of AI in emerging markets also opens the door for companies here to provide new services and products to the same, utilizing AI as the delivery channel. AI-compatible agricultural tools are almost automatically a popular offering, for example. With fewer and fewer people in rural areas, automation makes more sense where harvests have to be taken care of so as to make it to the next growing cycle. AI channels can also solve health demands, education issues, and financial services concerns in these same markets. And the objective automation of AI helps keep a limit on human-related mistakes or errors too.

Exploring AI-Driven Business Models

A big disruptor coming online that can be implemented by companies of all sizes includes AI-driven business models. These are monetization channels based on providing access to AI on a subscription basis. Customers can easily afford a subscription when they otherwise could not afford capital expenses for buying the tool outright. This produces long-term revenue channels from consistent customers that become dependent on AI for their own businesses in emerging markets.

That said, just disrupting without a plan ends up being a mistake. A strategic approach to applying disruptive market entry is necessary, especially when demand goes viral for the new service or product. An entry and implementation strategy anticipates the market change and then provides the means to support innovation, much the same way tool merchants helped gold miners obtain what they needed in the gold rush.

Breakthrough Applications

AI functions aggressively as a catalyst for new software application development. And it doesn't discriminate by industry. All are welcome.

AI in Space Exploration and Commercialization

The aerospace industry is growing left and right with AI as well. Automated control that functions within multiple variables and a wide set of parameters makes it very possible to operate equipment without human operators needing to be involved. That's particularly useful in high-risk ventures such as outer space and similar environments that aren't easy for people to work in normally. It won't be surprising to see AI applied in space harvesting when industry capabilities become a reality in the next decade. Remember, Earth isn't the only planet to have minerals. AI combined with robotics opens the door for harvesting on everything from asteroids to Mars.

Advancing Personalized Medicine and Healthcare

As mentioned earlier, AI is a groundbreaking push forward for medicine, and healthcare benefits from the same. The ability to crunch protein samples and find possibilities that otherwise took months and instead do the same in a day puts research in light-speed mode. That translates to faster medical discoveries, which in turn improves healthcare faster for a lower cost. It's a chain reaction of benefits for industries, medical providers, and patients.

Health-related businesses can position themselves at the front line of the next healthcare market wave with AI, especially as it personalizes into 24/7 care with AI and automation. Patient monitoring, lower cost of delivery, and better patient results all become a measurable reality from the technology.

Preparing for Market Disruptions
Risk Management and Mitigation

AI's predictive value comes into vogue with risk management, especially with spotting other market disruptions that might be on the way.

Identifying and Addressing Potential AI Risks

AI works to the extent that it stays objective. The tool becomes faulty when the data it relies on has inherent biases. That in turn skews the results, which then skews decision-making. By keeping AI clean with its base data, companies that use the tool end up working with quality references. The downstream results turn out better and acknowledge real risks versus covering them up. When competitors see this, the adoption of AI begins to be reinforced. The way to make sure AI isn't being abused is to apply audits and regular monitoring as well as transparency requirements on how conclusions are arrived at based on AI.

Developing Comprehensive Contingency Plans

Like anything constructed, however, even AI can break down. Smart management will have a backup plan for decision-making support when that contingency occurs. Whether it be a security leak or AI provisioning failure, having a back-up plan provides redundancy when it matters most. By having a contingency plan in place, a business can be ready for the worst and enjoy the best of AI.

Agile and Adaptive Strategies

Strategies for AI use shouldn't be cast in stone, however. They should be flexible, periodically changeable, to address new AI evolutions as well as changing demands for its use.

Adopting Agile AI Development Practices

One of the more effective ways to keep improving AI implementation involves an agile approach to feedback and management adjustment. The approach allows a business to change quickly to shifts in the market as well as organizational performance. An agile approach also makes sure AI doesn't sit in a stovepipe in a company. Instead, cross-functional teams bring input from multiple perspectives, which fosters creativity and multiple uses of AI. In short, AI's relevancy increases with an agile approach.

Implementing Responsive AI Solutions

When agile feedback loops are combined with responsive AI, sparks fly. The technology works extremely well with fluid situations and changing variables. Rather than dealing with the problem of having to repeatedly rewrite static parameters, responsive AI changes on the fly. So, agile responses are far more meaningful and relevant to immediate needs. As the AI algorithms expand in capacity, a company's predictive capabilities for managing risk become far more effective as well.

Sustainable AI Practices

AI is revolutionizing business landscapes worldwide, particularly in emerging markets where resources and infrastructure are often limited. These regions, characterized by a high concentration of small businesses, entrepreneurs, and local networks, are finding AI to be a gamechanger. Much like cloud technology, AI provides unprecedented opportunities for growth by filling resource gaps and enabling innovative solutions that were previously out of reach.

AI's rise in these markets also offers new avenues for businesses to introduce products and services tailored to local needs, such as AI-driven agricultural tools, healthcare solutions, and educational platforms. Furthermore, AI-driven business models—like subscription-based services—present scalable and sustainable revenue streams, fostering long-term customer retention and market expansion.

However, successfully leveraging AI in these markets requires strategic planning. Companies must anticipate market disruptions and craft effective entry strategies, ensuring they are prepared to support rapid innovation. With AI catalyzing advancements across various sectors, from space exploration to personalized medicine, it becomes clear that its potential to reshape industries is boundless. To capitalize on these opportunities, businesses must adopt agile, adaptive strategies that align with evolving market dynamics and technological advancements.

Ensuring Long-Term AI Sustainability

An additional big question managers may have about AI involves its sustainability. With the tool changing so fast, how long is an investment in AI today good for? It's a critical consideration.

Investing in Green AI Technologies & Adopting Eco-Friendly AI Practices

The value of AI comes in its application. By linking AI to green business processes, even older versions of the tool can be applicable for years in terms of maintaining systems that are dedicated to reducing carbon emissions, slowing down waste, boosting recycling, and being eco-friendly. That easily comes in the form of facility management, for example. As AI evolves and becomes integrated, the eco-responsibility of the organization becomes a natural by-product.

Collaborative Innovation

As noted in previous sections, AI realizes greater benefits when combined with collaboration versus used in a silo.

Engaging in Multi-Stakeholder Partnerships

Looking at AI data and results from its analysis through multi-stakeholder perspectives helps catch omissions, oversights, missing data gaps, and incorrect logic applications. By combining AI with a multi-functional review instead, the capability of the tool can be refined, and the output can be quality-checked regularly. This approach leans heavily into transparency and the ethical use of AI, which adds to a business' goodwill and reputation applying AI. It also benefits recipients with a better service or product from the AI usage.

Directing Future AI Research and Development

By hitching AI usage and business process growth to sustainable goals, the automated aspects of AI can easily open additional opportunities for avoiding waste and boosting productivity. Socially, the application of the tool improves the overall reputation of the company externally, and internally employees see a greater dedication to reducing inefficiencies in the workplace. That drives an interest in being part of a greater good that benefits the company, the employees, and the community as a whole. The combination boosts the demand for AI research and development in doing more with AI toward bigger wins for everyone.

Future AI research won't happen on its own momentum; it needs demand to pull ideas into reality. When AI is combined with a purpose people already want to realize, the resulting development happens much faster with investment, support, and expectation.

Conclusion

The future of Generative AI is poised to redefine the landscape of business in fundamental ways. As organizations navigate the complexities of this evolving technology, strategic investments in emerging fields like quantum and neuromorphic computing will be critical. Businesses that embrace innovative AI paradigms, such as federated learning and explainable AI, are not just future-proofing themselves against painful disruption but also positioning their companies for competitive advantage in an increasingly data-driven world. This requires a broad and deep commitment to continuous learning, development, and the creation of scalable AI infrastructures that can adapt to rapid technological advancements.

Looking ahead, successful businesses will harness the full potential of AI by fostering collaborations, leveraging new market opportunities, and adopting agile and sustainable practices. By aligning AI strategies with both current needs and future possibilities, companies can unlock transformative growth while ensuring ethical and transparent use. Ultimately, preparing for the future of Generative AI is not merely about adopting new technologies—it's about reshaping organizational culture and capabilities to thrive in an era defined by intelligent automation and continuous innovation.

Index

A

Access controls, 136
Accountability, 52, 131, 139
Agile and adaptive strategies, 172, 173
AI, *see* Artificial intelligence (AI)
AI-assisted design, 91, 97
AI-Augmented Innovation Cycle, 96
AI chatbots, 76, 77
AI-driven business models, 170, 173
AI-driven demand forecasting, 76
AI-driven customer interactions, 67, 69
AI-driven learning programs, 165
AI ethics policies, 122
AI-generated code, 93
AI-generated content, 129
    accuracy, 132
    bias and fairness, 130, 131
    ownership, 129
    reliability, 132
    testing and validation, 132
AI-powered code-review tools, 93
AI-powered marketing, 95
AI-ready environments, 167, 168

AI-specific regulations, 135
AI strategy
    full-scale deployment, 110
    objectives, 109
    roadmapping implementation
        adaptability, 112
        benefits, 111
        change management, 112
        long-term vision, 112
        performance measurement, 112
        phased implementation, 111
        prioritization and resource allocation efficiencies, 111
        risk mitigation, 111
        stakeholder engagement, 112
        strategic alignment, 111
    strategic vision, 109
    use case identification
        feasibility assessment, 110
        high-impact use cases, 110
AI systems, 10, 66, 83, 98, 127, 131–133, 140, 152, 167, 168
Analytics tracking online behavior, 54
APIs, *see* Application programming interfaces (APIs)

© Ahmed Bouzid, Paolo Narciso, Weiye Ma 2024
A. Bouzid et al., *Generative AI For Executives*,
https://doi.org/10.1007/979-8-8688-0950-7

Application programming
    interfaces (APIs), 71, 93, 94
Artificial intelligence (AI), 1, 75, 87
    applications, 77, 80, 82
    deployment, 136, 147,
        150–152, 167
    generative, 1
    human intelligence and
        cognition, 2
    implementation, 101, 111, 172
    integration, 73, 107, 108
    liability, 135
    maturity, 107–108
    research and development, 175
    risks, 172
    software, 2
    traditional, 1
    transparency, 52, 135
    types, 3
Automation approach, 55

B

Business expertise, 117, 119
Bias detection, 123
BLEU scores, 151
Business executives
    continuous monitoring,
        143, 144
    legal and ethical considerations,
        142, 143
    risk assessments, 141
    risk management, 142
Business impact, 151, 153

Business opportunities
    advancing personalized
        medicine, 171
    AI in emerging markets
        AI-driven business
            models, 170
        opportunity, 169
        untapped market
            segments, 169
    AI in space exploration and
        commercialization,
        170, 171
    healthcare, 171

C

California Consumer Privacy Act
    (CCPA), 70, 98, 126,
        128, 133
Canadian Personal Information
    Protection and Electronic
    Documents Act (PIPEDA),
        126, 129
CBDAS data maturity model, 150
CCPA, *see* California Consumer
    Privacy Act (CCPA)
Change management, 80, 112,
        120, 121
Cloud networks, 166, 167
Collaborative innovation, 174, 175
Competitor pricing analysis, 17
Compliance
    cost consideration, 137
    frameworks, 138

and legal teams, 138
    mechanisms, 124
    regulatory compliance, 137, 138
Concept development, 97
Conditional generation, 9
Consumer protection laws, 134
Content creation, 40, 94, 153, 154
Contingency planning, 142
Contingency plans, 172
Continuous improvement, 50, 97
Continuous monitoring, 143,
    144, 153
Copyright, 130, 134
Cross-border data transfer, 135
Cross-functional teams, 117, 173
    collaboration, 119
    diversity, 119
    team composition, 119
Culture of innovation, 105
    change management, 120, 121
    encouraging experimentation,
    121, 122
    leadership commitment, 120
Customer data, 63, 70, 95
Customer interactions, 67, 68
    generative AI solutions, 60
    personalization and
    responsiveness, 59, 61
Customer journey, 68
Customer satisfaction, 35, 61,
    63–65, 101
Customer sentiments, 26
Customer service, 63–67, 69, 73, 77
Customer support, 55

D

Data scientists, 4, 116–118
Data accuracy, 137
Data breaches, 127
Data classification, 136
Data collection, 114
Data encryption, 136
Data governance
    and data management, 136
    data quality and integrity, 137
Data infrastructure, 76, 77,
    100, 106–107
Data integrity, 137
Data management, 113
    access controls, 136
    data classification, 136
    data collection, 114
    data encryption, 136
    data processing, 115
    data storage, 114
Data privacy, 49, 98, 155
Data privacy and security
    data handling and protection,
    127, 128
    data protection regulations,
    128, 129
Data processing, 115, 128, 163
Data protection laws, 133
Data protection regulations,
    126, 128–129
Data quality, 137
Data storage, 114
Decision-making, 24, 25, 44

Derivative works, 129
Diverse data, 123

E

Eco-friendly AI practices, 174
Emerging AI trends
    federated learning, 162
    neuromorphic computing, 161
    quantum computing, 160, 161
    technology investment, 160
    XAI, 162, 163
Empowering marketing teams, 46
    anxiety, 46
    marketing processes, 48
    mistakes, 47
    protection, 50
    seamless transition, 49
    tool paradigm, 47
    two-step assessment, 48
Ethical AI framework, 143
Ethical and social impact metrics,
        152, 154
Ethical concerns, 51, 69, 126, 130,
        138, 139
Ethical framework, 139
Ethical guidelines, 52, 122, 139
Ethical principles, 143, 155
Ethical review, 122
Ethical review boards, 139
Ethics committees, 143
Evaluation, Generative AI
    baseline measurements, 153
    BLEU, 151

business impact metrics, 151
CBDAS data maturity
        model, 150
challenges, 147, 155
content creation, 153, 154
continuous monitoring, 153
ethical and social impact
        metrics, 152
evaluation framework, 152
futures, 155, 156
GreatAI framework, 150
long-term strategic metrics, 152
metrics, 150–152
multifaceted nature, 148
periodic assessments, 153
response time, 151
revenue impact
        assessments, 151
Social Impact Evaluation
        Framework, 149
Sociotechnical Evaluation
        Framework, 148–149, 153
technical performance, 151
user experience metrics, 151
Executive support, 120
Explainable AI (XAI), 160, 162–163

F

Fashion retailer, 65–66
Feasibility assessment, 110
Federated learning, 162
Feedback loops, 50, 53, 81, 144
Future of Generative AI

emerging AI trends, 160–163

market disruptions, 171–173

scalable AI
infrastructure, 166–169

sustainable AI
practices, 173–175

workforce, 163–166

G

GANs, *see* Generative adversarial
networks (GANs)

GDPR, *see* General Data Protection
Regulation (GDPR)

General Data Protection
Regulation (GDPR), 70, 98,
128, 133

Generative adversarial networks
(GANs), 8, 61

Generative AI, 2, 3, 5, 6, 17, 20, 21,
29, 30, 37–39, 45, 48, 50, 53,
54, 59, 60, 62, 65, 76, 78, 83,
88–90, 96, 98, 100, 102, 103

adoption, 63

applications, 94

business executive, 11

business functions, 14

capacity, 6

ChatGPT, 7

competitors, 17

conditional generation, 9

customer care and support, 18

customer revenue growth, 12

on customer service, 65

data, 10

datasets, patient records, 7

drug research and
discovery, 8

employee disengagement, 15

financial chores, 15

financial records, 15

GANs, 8

generative, 67

hyperparameter, 11

marketing
communications, 17, 18

marketing landscape, 94

NLP, 9

operational benefits, 84

pricing, 16

product design and
prototyping, 91

product development, 93

product features and
offerings, 20

prototyping, 92

recruitment, 13

sales success, 11

scores, 12

supervised learning, 10

synthetic medical images, 7

talent retention, 13

team member's knowledge, 14

testing, 93

tools, 88, 91

transfer learning, 9

unsupervised learning, 10

visual design, 91

Generative AI solutions, 68, 78, 79
  AI integration, 82
  AI models, 79
  feedback loops, 81
  infrastructure, 79
  innovative applications, 82
  job descriptions, 82
  job displacement, 81
  learning and AI adoption, 80
  pilot projects, 79
  technology vendor, 79
  upskill staff, 80
Generative AI tools, 101
Global AI research entities, 169
GreatAI framework, 150
Green AI technologies, 174

H

Healthcare, 78, 162, 171
Hiring AI experts, 116–118

I, J

Identify risks
  business executives, 141–144
  data privacy and
    security, 126–129
  ethical concerns, 126, 130, 131
  IP issues, 126, 129, 130
  operational risks, 127, 132, 133
Implementation, Generative AI
  AI maturity assessment,
    107, 108

AI strategy, 109–113
bias detection, 123
culture of innovation, 120–122
data infrastructure, 106
diverse data, 123
ethical guidelines, 122
gap analysis
  process gaps, 108
  skills gaps, 108
  technology gaps, 108
industry analysis, 106
infrastructure assessment, 106
investing in technology
  infrastructure, 113–116
minimizing bias, 123
regulatory
  compliance, 123, 124
skilled workforce, 116–119
software ecosystem, 107
speed and nature, 106
Industry collaborations, 168
Infrastructure assessment, 106
Innovation encouragement, 121
Integration plan, 116
Intellectual property (IP) issues,
  126, 129, 130
Intelligent automation, 76
International Regulations and
  Standards, 134
Internet of Things (IoT)
  networks, 166–168
Inventory management, 29
IoT networks, *see* Internet of Things
  (IoT) networks

IP issues, *see* Intellectual property (IP) issues
IP laws, 134
ISO Standards, 134

K

Key operational domains, 76
Key performance indicators (KPIs), 49, 50, 101, 112
Knowledge sharing, 102, 119
KPIs, *see* Key performance indicators (KPIs)

L

Large language models (LLMs), 87, 88, 90
Launch planning, 95, 96
Leadership commitment, 120
Legal adaptation, 144
Legal and compliance teams, 138
Legal and ethical considerations
    ethical AI framework, 143
    legal experts, 142, 143
Legal and regulatory landscape, 144
Legal consultations, 138, 142
Legal developments, 134
Legal experts, 142–143
Legal frameworks, 126, 133, 135
Legal frameworks and regulations
    International Regulations and Standards, 134

legal developments, 134, 135
legal landscape, 133, 134
Legal reviews, 143
Legal trends, 135
Legislation, 133, 135, 137
LLMs, *see* Large language models (LLMs)
Long-term AI sustainability, 174

M

Machine learning, 7, 11, 75, 78
Market disruptions
    agile and adaptive strategies, 172, 173
    risk management and mitigation, 171, 172
Market expansions, 30–31
Marketing analysis, 54
Marketing teams, 47, 48, 56
Market segments, 169–170
Mitigating risks
    compliance, 137, 138
    data governance, 136, 137
    ethical concerns, 138, 139
    operational resilience, 140
Multi-stakeholder partnerships, 175

N

Natural language processing (NLP), 9, 26, 75, 150
Neuromorphic computing, 161
NLP, *see* Natural language processing (NLP)

O

OECD Principles on AI, 134
Ongoing monitoring, 140, 144
Operational efficiency, 27–28, 76
Operational resilience, 140
Operational risks, 127, 132, 133
Organizational culture, 108

P

Patents, 130
Performance measurement, 112
Performance monitoring, 140
Periodic assessments, 153
Periodic audits, 50, 53
Periodic reviews, 140
Personalization, 40–41, 54, 61–63, 66, 95, 96
Personalized engagement, 64–65
Personalized financial advice, 66
Personalized medicine, 171, 174
PIPEDA, *see* Canadian Personal Information Protection and Electronic Documents Act (PIPEDA)
Predictive analysis, 7, 24, 54
Privacy compliance tracking, 152
Product development lifecycle, 88, 96
Product innovation, 30, 31, 98, 103
Prompt-driven A/V content, 56
Prototype creation, 97
Public–private partnerships, 166, 168

Q

Quality scores, 154
Quantum computing, 160–161

R

Real-time monitoring, 112, 144
Regular audits, 53, 70, 100, 137
Regulatory awareness, 123
Regulatory compliance, 123–124, 137, 138
Regulatory development, 57
Regulatory updates, 144
Resource allocation, 25, 28, 32, 35, 78, 111, 155
Responsible AI, 52, 101, 122, 139, 143
Returns on investment (ROI), 40, 84
Risk assessments, 141
Risk identification, 141
Risk management, 29, 30, 142
and mitigation, 111, 141, 171–172
Robust AI systems, 140
ROI, *see* Returns on investment (ROI)

S

Scalable AI infrastructure
AI-ready environments, 167, 168
business opportunities, 169–171

cloud networks, 166
global AI research entities, 169
industry collaborations, 168
industry-wide
standardization, 166
IoT networks, 166
public–private partnerships,
166, 168
Skilled workforce
cross-functional teams, 117, 119
knowledge sharing, 119
talent acquisition, 116–118
training and
development, 117–119
training programs, 118
Skill gaps, 71, 133
Skills assessment, 118
Smart-home app, 94
Smart-home system, 95, 96
Smart infrastructures, 166, 167
Smart management, 172
Social Impact Evaluation
Framework, 149
Social media, 25, 89, 95, 126
Sociotechnical Evaluation
Framework, 148–149, 153
Software ecosystem, 107
Space exploration, 170–171, 174
Stakeholder engagement, 112, 121
Strategic alignment, 108, 111
Streamline operations, 76, 84
Supervised learning, 10
Supply chain management, 28,
34, 76, 77

Support structures, 122
Sustainable AI practices
AI-driven agricultural tools, 173
cloud technology, 173
collaborative innovation,
174, 175
long-term AI sustainability, 174
strategic planning, 174

T

Talent acquisition, 116–118
Talent management, 163, 164
Talent recruitment, 118
Technical performance
metrics, 153
Technology infrastructure
AI tools and platforms, 113, 115
data management, 113–115
integration with existing
systems, 114–116
Technology investment, 160
Testing and validation, 116, 132
Traditional AI, 3, 5, 59, 60, 62
financial regulations and
policies, 5
and generative AI, 4, 63
real-time decisions, 5
setting, 5
software, 3
Traditional marketing, 50
Training programs, 80, 101,
117, 118
Training teams, 58, 165

Transfer learning, 9

Transformative potential
    assisting business executives, 33
    bridges, 25
    business executive, 23
    collaboration, 32
    collaborative processes, 32
    collaborative work
        environments, 31
    communication, 33
    content generation, 43
    creativity, 56
    customer feedback, 36
    customer insights, 25
    data analysis and decision-
        making, 24
    in-time collaboration, 25
    marketing approaches, 40
    marketing campaign, 40
    marketing position, 41
    marketing team, 42, 52
    operational efficiency, 28
    operational processes, 34
    outcomes, 29
    performances, 34
    potential catalyst, 35
    product and process
        innovation, 31, 35–36
    professional production, 41
    resource allocation, 25
    schedules and resource
        allocation, 35
    teams and marketing
        support, 43
    traditional marketing, 40
    virtual cost-cutting partner, 33

Transparency, 70, 131, 135,
    139, 162

Transparent practices, 139

U

Unauthorized access, 128
Unsupervised learning, 10
User-centric evaluation, 156
User experience metrics, 151, 154

V

Vision communication, 120

W, X, Y, Z

Workforce
    AI-driven learning
        programs, 165
    AI skills into training
        curricula, 165
    continuous learning and
        development, 165
    new AI-centric job
        opportunities, 164, 165
    responsibilities, 163
    roles with AI integration, 164
    talent management, 163, 164

GPSR Compliance

The European Union's (EU) General Product Safety Regulation (GPSR) is a set of rules that requires consumer products to be safe and our obligations to ensure this.

If you have any concerns about our products, you can contact us on

ProductSafety@springernature.com

In case Publisher is established outside the EU, the EU authorized representative is:

Springer Nature Customer Service Center GmbH
Europaplatz 3
69115 Heidelberg, Germany